P9-ECR-405

Which Tribe Do You Belong To?

Alberto Moravia

Which Tribe Do You Belong To?

*Translated from the Italian
by Angus Davidson*

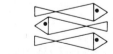

Farrar, Straus and Giroux
New York

Published in Italian under the title *A Quale Tribù Appartieni?*
copyright © 1972 by Casa Editrice Bompiani & C.S.p.A.
English translation copyright © 1974 by Martin Secker & Warburg Limited
Acknowledgment is made to the editors of *Antaeus, Oui,* and *Harper's Magazine,* in which portions of this book originally appeared.
First American printing, 1974
Printed in the United States of America

Library of Congress Cataloging in Publication Data

Moravia, Alberto.
    Which tribe do you belong to?
    Translation of A quale tribù appartieni?
    1. Africa, Sub-Saharan—Description and travel.
  I. Title.
DT352.M6613   1974   916.7'04   74-5316

Contents

1

Fashions in Clothes at Accra

Accra, March 1963

From the balcony of my room I had a panoramic view over Accra, capital of Ghana. Beneath a sky of hazy blue, filled with mists and ragged yellow and grey clouds, the town looked like a huge pan of thick, dark cabbage soup in which numerous pieces of white *pasta* were on the boil. The cabbages were the tropical trees with rich, trailing, heavy foliage of dark green speckled with black shadows; the pieces of *pasta* the brand-new buildings of reinforced concrete, numbers of which were now rising all over the town. One of these buildings was my hotel, which stood in the middle of a big park all aflame with red flowers. It was an enormous, very recent construction, built in a colourful, picturesque style that might be called 'neo-African'. In this hotel there were colonnades with groups of chairs and little tables where one could sit and consume good iced drinks; there was a vast dining-room with big glazed windows, the room being painted in tones of periwinkle blue and cream yellow and spotlessly clean, each table sparkling with polished cutlery and shining glasses, and with African waiters dressed as though for an eighteenth-century ballet; there was a large bar with a high, massive counter like an altar; there was a spacious, comfortable lounge; there was an all-metal lift rising to the wide, well-ventilated, luminous corridors of the upper floors; there were rooms very luxuriously fitted up, bathrooms with porcelain tiles of the best quality on floors of plastic material, curtains of tropical fabrics and light, modern furniture.

When had this hotel been built? Only a short time ago,

since Gunther, in his book about Africa, spoke of Accra, in 1954, in these somewhat unflattering terms: 'a jumble of tin huts mixed with decrepit buildings of beams and brickwork, with wretched, mean little shops beneath crumbling arcades. A spectator's first impression is of an almost hopeless squalor . . .' Two or three years ago, perhaps. In any case, as already mentioned, this was not the only modern building in Accra. A brief visit to the new part of the town reveals ministerial offices in the most modern style, raised on reinforced concrete piles, with long verandas of colonial type sheltering the doors leading to rooms where, amongst Swedish-type furniture, officials in short-sleeved shirts and white trousers examine documents, aided by female secretaries who are invariably attractive and well-dressed; white suburban houses buried amongst dark, frowning tropical greenery, and villas in contrasting colours with recessed porticoes.

The streets of this residential part of Accra wind through gardens that are as exuberant and full of flowers as the avenues of a large public park; and in these streets few passers-by are to be seen, but numbers of American and English cars.

The shanty town of which Gunther spoke still, of course, exists, beside the luxurious modern town. Ten minutes by car from my hotel, the asphalt of the streets turns into a yellowish dirt, and the concrete buildings in an orderly row along the pavements are succeeded by innumerable huts and shacks grouped like mushrooms at the edges of the rough unmetalled roads. And the centre of Accra is certainly not modern: a wide, ramshackle street, like that of some little town in the Far West, with two rows of heterogeneous, uneven buildings, here a modern block all made of glass, there a hut with a corrugated-iron roof, farther on a long two-storeyed building, and beyond that even a shack with a roof of thatch. And, along the pavements, alternating with parking-places chock-full of cars, open-air markets with their goods displayed on the ground and, amongst the merchandise, the market-women, all of them enormously corpulent, sheltering under great straw hats and with their thighs overflowing the sides of their minute stools.

Between these two towns, one of them modern and luxurious, the other decrepit and wretched, there is a complete lack of any kind of intermediate zone of residential quarters of a middle-class type; just as, not only in Accra but in the whole of Africa, there has been an entire absence of any transition phase between the colonialism of yesterday and the neo-capitalism of today. There has been a change from pith-helmeted military men to grey-clad bankers, from the atavistic hut to the skyscraper – abruptly, without transition. The young official working in up-to-date, air-conditioned offices has, perhaps, a father who lives in a hut in the prairie and drives his flocks to pasture with a shepherd's crook in one hand and a spear in the other to defend himself against wild beasts.

What all this implies is that neo-capitalism is flinging itself upon Africa with the speed and violence with which fire seizes upon a substance that is both very dry and very greasy. The hotel at Accra, for instance, is but one of the large number of similar hotels which have arisen more or less everywhere in the Black Continent, from the Atlantic to the Indian Ocean. Side by side with these hotels, in the modern quarters of the African towns, there have appeared numbers of buildings that testify to the interest of large-scale European and American capital in Africa: haughty, gloomy, cold-looking bank premises of the same black, shining marble and close-grained, grey granite that is to be seen in Zurich, London, New York and Frankfurt; small pocket-sized skyscrapers of glass and metal with rows of brass nameplates at the doors on which you can read numerous inscriptions ending in the authoritative abbreviation 'Ltd'; centres of commerce with huge shop-windows, moving staircases and female assistants in uniform, as in the ten-cent stores of New York.

We have moved a long way, now, from the old colonialism, with its decaying bungalows, its Victorian hotels, its slave-owners' bars, its dusty shops and, indeed, its Conrad-like picturesqueness. Neo-capitalism, not in the least afraid

3

of malaria, of the tsetse fly, of damp heat or dry heat, of mud from the rains and dust in the dog days, of the backwardness and primitive state of the various peoples and of the lack of roads and towns, strengthened by the recent triumphant experiments in the spheres of machinery and of medicinal drugs, now feels itself capable of absorbing Africa much more rapidly and completely than over-populated Asia, or than Latin America, lethargic and blighted by its Spanish inheritance. The interest of neo-capitalism in Africa is, moreover, justified not only by the good labour-market and by the presence of the most diverse mineral wealth, but also by the rivalry with communism and by the need to act quickly in order to thwart all possibility of political revolution by means of a consumer revolution.

Others, furnished with statistics, will be able to state better than I how the neo-capitalist invasion of Africa stands today in terms of figures and operations. I myself am interested, if anything, in all those things which economists usually do not mention, that is, in certain aspects of this invasion which are less rational but not on that account less important. Yet there is no doubt that, whereas the red star of communism shines over Asia, it is – for the present at any rate – the white star of neo-capitalism that gleams over Africa. In other words, it seems that in this there are reasons of a historical, ethnical, psychological and aesthetic nature owing to which the African, faced by problems of economic underdevelopment and of social and cultural backwardness analogous to those of Asia, in contrast to the people of Asia who are either Marxists or at least tempted by Marxism, prefers, instead, to adopt Western solutions. Of these irrational motives there are, in the main, three: the first is colonialism which, just because it was stronger and more cruel here than elsewhere, drove the Africans into adopting the culture of those very same colonialists against whom they are rebelling; and this, partly, because it is in European culture that is to be found the most efficacious antidote to the evils which it has brought, and partly because of the relationship of attraction and repulsion that always establishes itself between the executioner and his

4

victim. The second motive is the individualistic character of African culture: Africa has never known the great centralizing, bureaucratic empires that have been so frequent in Asia; outside tribe and family, the African had always been as free as a bird in the air or a fish in the water. The third motive is the special character of the magical and fetishistic beliefs of Africa which are not an obstacle, as are the Asiatic religions, to the understanding and acceptance of industrial civilization, but rather a positive stimulus to such an understanding and acceptance, precisely because of the element of fetishism and magic that exists in machines. To these three motives can be added a fourth, whose origin lies in the childish character of the African: neo-capitalism, with the infinite number of mass-produced products of its light industry, all of them well-made, ingenious and almost all of them superfluous, fascinates Africans in the same way that they were fascinated by the brass and copper wire and the Venetian glass beads which the adventurers of a century or two ago offered them in exchange for gold, ivory and precious woods.

I was thinking over these matters as I walked along the main street of Accra, through the most multicoloured crowd I had ever seen in my life. It was a cheerful, unbelievable sight: between the ramshackle, uneven buildings of this principal street swarmed a multitude of people dressed in materials of the most dazzling colours and the boldest designs imaginable. The men wrap these materials round their bodies in the manner of Roman togas, from head to foot, leaving their necks and one shoulder and one arm bare. The women wind them tightly round their hips and breasts like evening dresses for La Scala or the Metropolitan; and a handkerchief of the same material is tied round their heads with enormous knots that make them look as though they were supporting vases of flowers. The materials, as I have already said, are of barbaric colour and design; but an expert eye cannot but detect that this barbaric quality is a second-degree product, that is, a barbarism that has filtered through the pictorial experiments of the European *avant-garde*. The little open-air markets display innumerable rolls of these materials, piled up on the pavements; I stopped and asked to be shown some of them. They are of very coarse cotton and the price is very low; one feels that, as a sort of compensation for this, the assemblage of such violent and such novel colours, of such extravagant, seductive designs, must have required a background of the cult of primitivism, of Gauguin, Cubism and *art nègre*. Manufactured in Manchester and in Holland, these materials interpret and at the same time stimulate the passion of the Africans for the brilliant colours which always have a very fine effect against a black skin.

As I walked, I admired the spectacle of all these men and women swaggering along the dusty road in the burning sunshine, with their togas and their evening dresses, giving an appearance of perpetual, frivolous festivity; and then a sudden recollection came to me: that of the printed cotton materials shown to me, during one of my Russian journeys, in the *kombinat* at Tashkent in Soviet Central Asia. Put beside the English and Dutch materials worn by the Africans of Accra, there is no doubt that the Soviet materials, printed in timid, old-fashioned colours and designs, would cut a very poor figure. So one is led to think that these materials, and in general all the products of Western light industry, have paved the way, in the psychological and cultural sense, for neo-capitalist influence in Africa; whereas the well-known dearth of light industry in the Soviet Union has had the opposite effect as regards the ideological and political expansion of communism. Man, certainly, does not live by coloured materials and other similar products alone; nor yet by bulldozers, tractors, turbines and mechanical excavators. And, to judge by the pleasure and the relish with which the inhabitants of Accra drape these variegated materials round their persons, it might be said that, in this part of the world at least, light industry brings greater satisfactions to man than heavy industry.

2

Fear in Africa

Lagos, March 1963

Sometimes I have asked myself the question: is Black Africa, in the historical sense, older or younger than Europe? On careful consideration, Europe – in comparison with primitive Africa, an Africa that is still wrapped in the cocoon of nature – Europe, which came out of that cocoon a long time ago, should be the older. On the other hand, however, there is no difficulty in realizing that Black Africa is at a cultural stage which was precisely that of Europe some thousands of years ago; so then it is Africa that is older. But Africa is only now approaching the industrial civilization which has been established in Europe for two centuries, therefore Africa is younger. Nevertheless it cannot be denied that the African does not understand the profound meaning of this industrial civilization; he accepts it without comprehending it and he fails to comprehend it because his religious conceptions are not only earlier than Calvinism, which lies at the source of this civilization, but actually earlier than Christianity itself; therefore Africa is older. But is it not perhaps true that the African is younger than the European in that he is more irrational, more thoughtless, more childish, more given to dancing and singing and play-acting, that is, to art forms which do not demand intellectual maturity, and so on? In reality, when all is said and done, Africans are at the same time both young and old – that is, the culture of Africa is archaic, yet at the same time its grafting into the modern world is still problematical and immature.

After remaining for thousands of years firmly rooted in this kind of culture, the Africans are today moving, by a headlong leap, into an industrial, neo-capitalist culture. Thus a journey in Africa, when it is not a mere dull excursion from one to another of those big hotels that the inhabitants of the Western world have strewn across the Black Continent, is a veritable dive into prehistory.

But what *is* this prehistory that so fascinates Europeans? First of all, it should be said, it is the actual conformation of the African landscape. The chief characteristic of this landscape is not diversity, as in Europe, but rather its terrifying monotony. The face of Africa bears a greater resemblance to that of an infant, with few barely indicated features, than to that of a man, upon which life has imprinted innumerable significant lines; in other words, it bears a greater resemblance to the face of the earth in prehistoric times, when there were no seasons and humanity had not yet made its appearance, than to the face of the earth as it is today, with the innumerable changes brought about both by time and by man. This monotony, furthermore, displays two truly prehistoric aspects: reiteration, that is, the repetition of a single theme or motif to the point of obsession, to the point of terror; and shapelessness, that is, the complete lack of limitation, of the finite, of pattern and form, in fact.

Prehistoric, for example, is the prairie which girdles Africa for thousands of kilometres from west to east, that is, from the Atlantic to the Indian Ocean. This prairie is a limitless steppe of a pale green colour dotted here and there, as far as the eye can see, with one single kind of tree, the small African acacia, bristling with thorns, with branches like an umbrella; and with one single kind of round, dark green shrub. One drives on and on by car, on roads or tracks, for hundreds of kilometres, and the steppe goes on for ever, it merely repeats itself with the two features that belong to it, the acacia and the shrub.

In the far distance, sometimes, in those remote solitudes, one can distinguish myriads of black specks moving rapidly through the swarm of acacias and shrubs: these are herds of zebra or gazelle fleeing to some unknown place, frightened by something unknown. If one stops in the middle of the prairie, the hum of the car engine is suddenly succeeded by a virginal, breathless silence, truly prehistoric in its depth and transparency. One hears a muted sound of wind; the sunlight floods the immense plain with implacable brilliance; all at once one feels one is being observed and discovers the small, sharp-eyed heads of some giraffes protruding, motionless, on the end of enormous necks, above the umbrella-like acacias. These timid, curious animals stand here and there amongst the trees and taller than the trees; then, at a gesture or the sound of a voice they flee away, crossing the road one after another in slow, awkward, heavy bounds, with their immensely long legs and massive bodies. We drive on again, and again the prairie starts repeating, millions and millions of times over and over again, for thousands of kilometres, its theme of the acacia and the shrub. Every now and then the plain appears to rise a little towards the sky and to form an outline of long, gentle hills that seem ready to enclose it and give it the shape of a wide valley; but it is a vain attempt which invariably disappears and dissolves into the usual formlessness.

Prehistoric, too, is the rain forest which extends immediately beyond the prairie and which also continues for thousands of kilometres; it also is of one single colour, uninterruptedly pale green in the plain but, in the forest, black. I drove through the forest, for instance, by the road which, in Nigeria, goes from Lagos to the legendary Benin, formerly the seat of marvellous sculptors and craftsmen. The road is narrow, straight, made of earth red as blood; you might think the forest was an expanse of black flesh across which a long wound, still open and still living, had been cut. Here again, one drives for hundreds and hundreds of kilometres without any change in the landscape: the forest, like the prairie, merely repeats itself, to the point of obsession. The predominant theme is the black tangle of trees and bushes, of lianas and creepers, rising like a wall on either side of the road and almost cutting off any sight of the sky, which is reduced to a blue streak parallel to the red streak of the road.

This tangle, at first sight, looks very varied and rich in

9

branching trees and trunks and dangling boughs; but the variety, again, repeats itself and finally the eye becomes satiated and ceases to examine and appreciate it. If one stops suddenly in the forest, here again one is struck by the virginal quality and the transparency of the silence. The forest rises straight up on either side of the road; a stream, black, putrid and motionless, penetrates in amongst the trees; here and there on the banks of this shallow, muddy water can be seen huge tree-trunks that have fallen from sheer old age and are decaying in peace, the eternal, death-like peace of the prehistoric age. The forest is funereal, gloomy, mute and empty; and it seems that nothing exists in the forest but snakes and insects. The forest, too, like the prairie, appears now and then to be seeking to emerge from its shapelessness and to show signs of something finite, recognizable, something with a form of its own, such as a clearing, a path, an isolated tree, a group of trees; but almost immediately this suggestion disintegrates and disappears in the green, dark shapelessness of the equatorial vegetation.

Prehistory in Africa exists not only in the conformation of the landscape but also in the universal presence of the one truly autochthonous religious belief – magic. In Europe the world of magic survives in modest and enigmatic remnants, like scraps of flotsam in the sea after a shipwreck; but in Africa one is all the time aware that the world of magic is still complete, intact and in working order. Now the world of magic is none other than the 'Africa sickness', no longer seen from the point of view of Europeans but from that of the Africans themselves. The 'Africa sickness' is a spell with a basis of fear, and this fear is the fear of prehistory, that is, of the irrational forces which in Europe man has succeeded in repelling and dominating during many thousands of years, but which here in Africa are, instead, still intrusive and uncontrolled. It is a fear to which the European finally becomes accustomed, partly because he has his roots elsewhere and his personality is sounder and less unstable than that of the African; it is a fear, in fact, that is painfully agreeable. But the fear of the African, who has no historical background, whose personality is flickering as the light of a candle, is a serious fear, a nameless fright, a perpetual, vague terror. Magic is the expression of this prehistoric fear; it is as foul and gloomy and demented as the 'Africa sickness' is aphrodisiac, even if disruptive and destructive. The truth is that magic is the other face of the 'Africa sickness'.

In the market at Lagos, where the sultriness was damp and tainted like that of a monstrous pile of washing, I picked my way through several passages between counters and stalls overflowing with merchandise and with foodstuffs all equally softened by their exposure to the noxious tropical heat; then, all of a sudden, I came upon an open space surrounded by huts, in which was displayed, on counters and on the ground, a kind of merchandise that attracted my attention. This was the so-called *ju-ju*, in other words, the objects used by the Africans for the innumerable operations of their magic, objects that can be bought in the market and that must be much sought-after, for in that open space there were at least twenty stall-holders all of them offering the same infernal goods. And what may this *ju-ju* be? First of all, there was a large number of big smoked rats, arranged in two rows and strung together on sticks like the figs of Calabria; then, in a large basket, a lot of dried chameleons; finally, lying on the counters, dishes and small baskets full of repellent bits and pieces upon which one's eye is afraid to dwell – skulls of monkeys and dogs and horses; feet of gazelles and antelopes; eyes, hoofs and bristles; clay discs, rods; pieces of excrement and other fragments, putrefied and unrecognizable. All this filth has its own significance, its own destination, its own price, its own usefulness. An African goes to the market, buys a rat or a skull or a chameleon, then takes it home and makes use of it for the operations of white or black magic, that is, benignant or malignant. And in what way? Why should one wish to know? Suffice it to say that he makes use of it and that he believes in it.

There can be recognized in *ju-ju* a very special quality of foulness, which is at the same time extravagant and repugnant and is of the very essence of fear. A sombre, disgusting substitute for science, *ju-ju* deceives itself into thinking that it controls fear whereas in reality it is the direct expression of it. The same can be said of the masks which, in certain areas of Black Africa, still today give an appearance of perpetual, sinister carnival to the life of the Africans. These masks have by now become very well known; there is hardly a drawing-room in Paris or London that does not have its African mask hanging on the wall. I shall confine myself to recalling just one of them among so many. In a large, grimy meadow in the outskirts of Lagos I came upon a circle of idlers. I approached and saw that, to the sound of a wooden drum struck at both ends, with the palms of his hands, by a decrepit, skeleton-like old man, a masked figure was dancing, or rather leaping up and down, first on one foot and then on the other. The body of the masked figure was clothed in straw tied round his legs, his waist and his shoulders, so that it looked like a sheaf of corn that was dancing; his face was covered with a black silk stocking on which were sewn bunches of white shells. At each leap the straw moved and fell apart but did not reveal the body of the dancer, which thus did not appear to exist at all; and the bunches of shells rose upwards, allowing a glimpse, not of his face but of the smooth black silk of the stocking, with only his nose barely indicated, as occurs in certain highly stylized Negro sculptures. It was not, perhaps, an immediately terrifying mask; and yet in the end it became almost unbearable for me to look at it. This mask, in fact, was not intended to arouse fear; it *was* fear. The transience of the human being so feared by the Africans was expressed in the body transformed into a sheaf of corn. The face, enclosed in the stocking and covered with shells like a reef under the sea, was an allusion to the inability of man to show his face in competition with prolific, overpowering nature. Then, up above the meadow, almost grazing the corrugated-iron roofs of the huts that surrounded it, suddenly, with a deafening roar, a huge aeroplane flew over. But the spectators did not turn their heads, they did not look up at the sky: the whole of their attention was concentrated on the masked figure impersonating fear.

3

The Dances of the Africans

Lagos, April 1963

The Africans dance. Someone here in Lagos has told me that the workers in the shipyards sometimes improvise a dance to the engine rhythm of an excavator or a rock drill. To anyone who knows the simplicity of the music with which the Africans accompany their dances – drums beaten by the hands or even hand-claps or snapping of the fingers – this transformation of bulldozer into musical instrument will not appear so strange. But this piece of information has, anyhow, a significance of its own. In the first place, it goes to indicate an irresistible inclination to express in dancing not merely this or that more important experience, such for instance as agricultural work or sexual initiation, but the whole of life. In the second place, it leads us to understand that the African is the only one among the so-called primitives who is capable of fitting happily – in fact actually by dancing – into modern industrial civilization.

With regard to this second quality only a few words are needed. There are primitive people in all five continents who translate the religious and social manifestations of their existence into dance; but it is only the African who has succeeded in becoming a modern man while still preserving intact his original dancing capacity. Furthermore, it must be said that the dance is merely the most striking aspect of the contagious primitive rhythm which the African has introduced into the modern world. This rhythm, which now seems to us an indivisible, ingrained part of industrial civilization, comes, on the contrary, straight from pre-historic, archaic times. It is the most precious gift that

Africa has given to humanity and, at the same time, it is the clearest sign of the influence of the Africans on contemporary habits.

As for the first quality, that of translating the whole of life into dance, it must be said that it is one of those obvious things which, just because they are so obvious, escape attention. And yet the phenomenon is not all that simple. I remember, for instance, one day when I was driving along the road that goes from Lagos to Benin – the streak of red earth between two vertical walls of black forest. Suddenly we saw, in the distance, a group of Africans walking in the middle of the road, dressed in their usual fluttering, multicoloured togas or tunics. They were walking quietly along, with the untiring, eager, carefree gait habitual with Africans when, with no apparent goal in view, they tramp across the boundless spaces of their continent. However, when we came within a short distance of the group, a tall, slim young man started a preliminary dance step, moving a little apart from the others. His companions did not even look at him but went on walking, chattering and laughing as they went. But suddenly a woman, also, began to dance as she walked along; then another young man; then another woman; and finally the whole group, as though by some sort of contagion or automatic imitation, came forward along the road, through the solemn, funereal solitude of the forest, leaping, waving their arms and swaying their hips, with a frenzy and violence which their quiet demeanour of a few minutes before had made it quite impossible to foresee.

We passed close beside them. There was an old man who carried, slung over his shoulder, a small wooden drum, the ends of which he struck with the palms of his hands; there were a few young men with pieces of fluttering, coloured materials thrown over their shoulders; finally there were some boys and some almost naked little girls. They were all dancing as they walked, their agitated movements in strange contrast with the absolute motionlessness of the forest; and the blank look in the eyes of all of them, with a fixed, preoccupied stare, gave the impression of an ecstasy that was both facile and, so to speak, always ready to shatter the thin diaphragm of individuality and bring man into communication with mystery. In this case the mystery was there, only two steps away, visible and obsessive: the forest, majestic, hostile, in the depths of which they were wandering like the faithful in the nave of a cathedral. The group continued to dance as we left them behind. The road was perfectly straight, and after about half a kilometre I turned and looked: they were no longer dancing but had now started walking again at a normal pace.

What is it I wish to say by quoting this example? I wish to say what I have already said: that the African dances out his own life; for this reason there is always something surprising in his dance, something spontaneous, something unforeseeable. The African, in point of fact, does not know what awaits him in his dance, just as, in general, we do not know what awaits us in life. He seeks to move his body in a certain direction, according to a certain rhythm. Sometimes, moving in this way, he succeeds in entering upon a more general, a more ample rhythm which was flowing around him, so to speak, as a current in the sea flows round a fish swimming in it or a piece of wreckage floating upon it; and then he begins to dance. But sometimes his personal rhythm does not succeed in inserting itself into the universal rhythm, and then the African immediately ceases to dance and resumes his normal gait. But he tries nevertheless, he tries continually to enter, dancing, into the rhythm of the cosmos, with the determination and the patience of a water-diviner, of a man digging for gold.

Dancing, for the African, is also a means of associating himself, or rather of shedding his superficial individual form, and merging with other people, in the way that different pieces of different metals become merged in a single crucible. Again I remember, in this connection, a day when, returning from a trip to Ibadan, we were passing through the outskirts of Lagos. The road ran beside an uninterrupted row of hovels fantastically blackened and rotted with damp, of huts patched up with pieces of petrol-tins and boards taken from drawers, of low buildings colour-washed with red and with corrugated-iron roofs. Here and there, between one hovel and the next, there was an open piece of meadow covered with shabby grass, rough and wild-looking and very different from the soft grass of European suburbs.' In one of these meadows we saw an assemblage of people, so we stopped and went over to them. It was an entirely blue crowd, blue being the colour of the Yoruba, which is one of the four large tribes into which the population of Nigeria is divided. All these blue cloaks and togas, trousers, shirts, tunics, drawers and handkerchiefs formed a great patch of harsh, acid, chemical blue under the low, cloudy sky, in the framework of the red-painted huts and of the great trees, widespread and teeming with green foliage that was almost black. Amongst all this blue there floated, here and there, as though on a slightly troubled sea, faces, arms and black shoulders, black with the greasy, lustrous black of well-roasted coffee. We had barely time to get out of the car before the crowd rushed towards us, surrounded us, swallowed us up. A moment earlier we had been in a free open space; a moment later we were wedged in amongst the bodies of a hundred people. We had the smell of them in our nostrils, their sweat on our skins, their legs amongst our legs and their chests against ours; and hundreds of eyes were gazing greedily at us.

An elderly man with a small white skull-cap came forward and explained that it was a dance competition and that, if we wished to be present, we should be welcome. At this explanation I at once understood the look in all those eyes, of the shape and size of so many hardboiled eggs in the white of which a black yolk had been disclosed through a hole: a look that was, let me say, ecstatic and, in an inoffensive way, cannibalistic. And I also understood the sensation, from which I could not escape, of being sur-rounded and swallowed up not so much by a crowd as by a throbbing, warm body furnished with innumerable limbs and with an infinite number of eyes and yet single in itself. This body, or rather this momentary fusion of a number of bodies into one, was an effect of the dance. When we declined the invitation, the crowd, after pressing us closely and squeezing us and impregnating us with its smell and its sweat, returned into the open space with a vast movement like that of an ebb-tide, and there again, spontaneously, formed a circle round the dancers. As we got back into the car we were able to see, from a distance, a number of diabolical masked figures leaping and shaking and, all round them, a surge of black, woolly heads rhythmically swaying.

But for the Africans the dance has also the value of a purely individual manifestation; and anyone can assure himself of this by going into one of the many night-clubs whose violent neon lights blaze forth, in the sultry, sombre nights of the Gulf of Guinea, in the depths of the most popular quarters of Lagos. These night-clubs are generally in the open air; the cement platform opens out in the midst of a multitude of rickety, peeling little tubular tables and chairs; the band is located on a rostrum, against a confused, ragged background of huts and hovels. Yet when the band, with passion and authority, strikes up a 'twist' or a 'high-life', the spectator immediately forgets the casual poverty of the surroundings and cannot but be fascinated by the grace, the elegance, the self-possession, the rhythm, the intense expressiveness of the dancers. These tall, slim Africans, smothered in immense jackets and trousers, as soon as they have got the knack of the dance keep firmly to it, moving over the platform with a swaying, impassive, disembodied lightness. Their feminine partners, incredibly agile, supple and long in limb, with ankles and wrists of prodigious elegance, and heads whose already strikingly projecting jaws seem to be emphasized by their conical hair arrangements, twist and turn in front of them in a way which manages to be at the same time both completely chaste and completely sexual.

Where had I seen them before, these thin, thread-like, black, elegant figures, these heads, all eyes and mouth, the skin of which had the greasiness, the unevenness, the gloss and the dark colour of bronze? Why, of course, in the museum in the cases of which are exhibited the mysterious sculptures of the Benin artists. In Europe these sculptures sometimes give the impression of caricature. But here, in these Lagos night-clubs, one sees that they are realistic, in fact almost photographic. In the Gulf of Guinea it is nature that is expressionistic, subjective, delirious, caricaturist – not the artists. Men dance and, through the dance, express the extravagance of nature.

4

The Fate of the Africans is
to be Always Walking

Kano, April 1963

The Africans walk. I have travelled for thousands of kilometres in Black Africa, and everywhere, both in the wild and in the cultivated territories, I have seen single individuals or couples of a man and woman or small families, or again groups of ten or twenty persons of both sexes and all ages walking through terrifying solitudes, over the limitless wastes of the prairie with its profusion of identical trees or along the paths which, like tunnels, penetrate the gloomy, compact mass of the rain forest.

Where are they going, these migrant Africans? They never have the look of the vagabond or tramp or beggar who is going goodness knows where; nor does he know himself, since, wherever he goes, things do not change. The Negroes, instead, seem to know perfectly well where they are going, and indeed they do know. The Negro, in fact, always goes about his own business; that is, he moves mainly for economic, commercial, or subsistence reasons. For the most part the Africans go back and forth to the markets, and when they are not going to or returning from the markets they are going to pastures or fields or coming back from them; finally, they may also be moving for family or social or magical reasons; but if one takes a close look one will see that behind these reasons there is always an economic reason. For the Africans, given to dancing, eccentric, fantastic, and irrational as their methods may be, are one of the most contriving races in the world, even if their contrivances are often mere exchanges in kind and the buying and selling on a small scale of a very few products of domestic manufacture. Moreover, mere interest does not suffice to explain the Africans' frenzy for trading. In reality the African lives at the level of the instinct for self-preservation and thus, for him, trading is not a profession but an indispensable mode of existence.

Seen from this angle, Black Africa appears not so much as a medley of large and small states in imitation of the West and cut up, more or less, according to the boundaries of the former French and British colonies, as can be seen on the map, but rather as a single organism in which economic unity, as a counter-balancing and integrating force, acts in opposition to infinite tribal fragmentation. And this is not an affirmation based upon conjecture and deceptive observation, but rather upon the fact that in Black Africa the towns which are mercantile centres are in the middle of territories that do not coincide with, and anyhow overlap, the political boundaries. This, you may say, occurs also in Europe. That is true; but in Europe linguistic, political, military, religious and, indeed, historical realities have a concrete quality that confers, so to speak, a sacred character upon frontiers. In Africa, on the other hand, this concrete quality does not exist, since, as already observed, it is a question of nations formed upon the guide-rule of the colonies which, in turn, had been designated by the interested judgment of the European colonizers. And so it is that the markets, with the tracks and roads and the land and water communications that link them to the centres of habitation, are still today the only garment that man has been able to throw over the savage, archaic nudity of Black Africa.

The markets of Africa – beautiful and strange, and in which one feels as one visits them that their true function far surpasses that of buying and selling, and that without them human life in Africa would be utterly extinguished and would return to a bestial level – I have visited several of these markets, and always, everywhere, I have found the same feverish, excited, festive, panic atmosphere, like that of a fair which is at the same time a religious meeting, a political assembly, a magical reunion, a cultural exchange, an erotic outburst.

These markets are generally to be found in the middle of the towns, in fact they constitute their vital centres; and at first sight, with their rows of huts and hovels on both sides of the extremely narrow lanes, with their disorderly, shouting crowds, their stench and their filth, they form an almost intolerable contrast with the towns themselves, which are very often built in the European or even actually the American style, with real houses and large blocks and even small skyscrapers. But on brief reflection one becomes convinced that the contrast is only apparent. The towns *can*, in fact they *must*, be built in the European manner: it is right that it should be so, seeing that Black Africa has decided to become modern. But its heart remains the old African heart, and it is also right that this should be so, seeing that, even though it is modernizing itself, Africa wishes to remain faithful to itself. Now the heart of African towns, whether at Lagos or Accra, at Ibadan or at Kano, is the market; and the market, in spite of the blocks of buildings that surround it, keeps the character it had at the time when, instead of the big buildings, there was forest and prairie, the character, that is, of the single social centre of a chaotic, embryonic world besieged perpetually by sombre, pitiless nature.

At other times the market is to be found not in the centre of the town but outside it, far from the inhabited quarters, possibly because the town could not contain within its walls the excessive number of traders' installations and the torrential flood of buyers. I recall particularly one of these suburban markets in the neighbourhood of Kano, in the north of Nigeria, a large town with a very fine style of its own, partly barbaric, partly Arab, which, when seen from the minaret of the mosque, looks as round as a ball or a basin, in the midst of a limitless plain of a pale green, almost blue colour. This ball or basin is brick red; the uniformity of this red is broken only slightly, here and there, by the jade green of a garden or of a municipal water-tank.

The houses, on one floor, built of mud blended with straw and painted with the burnt sienna already mentioned, have smooth walls with an undulating surface, like petrified waves upon which, when the mud was still soft, sinuous furrows had been impressed with a pointed tool or a trowel, these also conveying the feeling of waves. These wave-like walls, their unbroken surfaces devoid of any opening save for the infrequent little door or minute window here and there, form narrow, deserted alleys in which the life of the African town reveals itself in all its terrible poverty: dust; a few naked children; a few women, huddled on doorsteps, pounding something or other in a mortar; a few men squatting in the sun amongst the flies. The silence is profound; the sun beats down between the embattled red walls from an immaculately blue sky. It is a vertical sun, hard and scorching, and it explains the hermetic quality of the town, an Arab quality, except that Arab towns are white whereas Kano is entirely red, the same colour, in fact, as, often, the earth of Africa.

Kano is a caravan town, to which there is a flow of people who wish to buy and people who wish to sell, coming from the most distant parts of Africa, both from west and east. A market was being held just that day about fifty kilometres from Kano, and to it we went. After an hour's drive, bumping over a sandy track, through the swarming shrubs and acacia trees of the prairie, we saw the first indications of this market: groups of Africans clothed in ample, fluttering garments of white cotton walking with that characteristically cheerful, peculiar step across the sandy waste, aiming for some unimaginable destination. At first there were only a few solitary individuals, then groups and families, and finally entire small crowds ambling along. They were walking hurriedly, chattering, laughing, gesticulating, with the anticipatory enthusiasm and expectant sociability natural to those who are on their way to a meeting-place where they know they will be swallowed up in a much greater multitude. Indeed all these Africans who were hurrying in small groups towards the market seemed already to be having a foretaste of the moment when they would plunge into the crowd and, mingling with a great number of others in the clouds of dust, in the sweat and the noise, would rid themselves of the unstable, troublesome superfluity of individual difference.

We reached the market, an immense expanse of flat ground with, here and there, great trees with heavy, spreading foliage and, under the trees, a multitude of people all dressed in white, like a crowd in an ancient Roman or Greek city. So flat was the plain that the crowd, with its white gestures and movements, stood out against the blue sky as though it were on the top of a mountain. Even from a distance one could see that this crowd was agitated by a violent jostling movement like that of different currents crossing each other in a stormy sea. It fluctuated, opened out and closed in again, came and went, wandered round, moved farther off and came back again. This was due to the movements of the places where business was being done; every now and then, in fact, when the crowd opened out, one caught a glimpse of a herd of oxen crammed close together, with endless numbers of short legs, endless numbers of black-nosed muzzles and of immense crescent-shaped horns. Then the crowd would close in again and above it I could see great black vultures circling slowly round as though seeking some prey and then returning to perch, their wings closed and their necks stretched out straight, on the branches of the trees. A thick dust rose above the crowd, darkening the air, a festive, joyful, exuberant, expansive kind of dust.

Then we went in among the crowd and walked about for two or three hours without stopping, in the inexhaustible amalgam of human beings which parted to let us through in a strange, automatic way of its own, as if, in making way for us and forming a narrow path for us between their bodies, the Africans had nevertheless not seen us, being as it were immersed in a kind of festive hypnosis. It is useless to try and describe the merchandise that was displayed on the ground, between the feet of the traders as they squatted over it. Whether it was the usual products of African gardens, whether it was the few objects of their own craftsmanship or perhaps goods mass-produced in America and Europe, what always struck one was not so much the merchandise as the men, both buyers and sellers. The merchandise was lacking in interest; but what the men contrived to do with these wretched things, what they derived from them apart from money, this was inexhaustible and always novel.

Such markets as these, as I have said, are scattered all over Black Africa. Africans start, let us say, from Senegal and then, by land or perhaps by river, reach Onitsha, on the Niger, not far from the river's mouth. If you look at the map you will see that this is a matter of some thousands of kilometres. These enormous distances that they face in order to sell or buy a few sacks of seed or a few dozen yards of cotton give a good idea of what the true Africa is, in contrast with the Africa of the maps. One thinks, not so much of a continent divided into nations, as of a great natural space, swarming with tribes but devoid of nationality, rather as Europe must have been during the Middle Ages, with its great fairs and its markets and the migrations from one fair to another, from one market to another. This characteristic of Black Africa, together with others whose description we are not concerned with here, encourages the prediction that Africa will become, not a multitude of big and small nations in the European manner, but a single large, unitary organism like the great continental countries such as India, China, the United States or the Soviet Union. The Africans walk; for their long, indefatigable legs space is needed.

5

The End of Courage

Arusha, May 1963

Hemingway has left us a picture of Africa which, with the end of colonialism on the one hand and the neo-capitalist invasion on the other, will soon become archaeological. As one travels in Africa one realizes the degree to which Hemingway's Africa 'dates', is bound up, that is, with a particular historical phase in the Black Continent. And Hemingway 'dates' not merely because he describes, in his African stories, a small society of snobs, of rich people, of failed intellectuals which now no longer exists, but also because the way of thinking that is apparent in his narrative is curiously antiquated and almost nineteenth-century. In stories such as *The Snows of Kilimanjaro* and *The Short Happy Life of Francis Macomber*, Hemingway gives us colonialism's moment of disappointment and bitterness; but he does not deviate from a scale of values which, *mutatis mutandis*, is still that of a Kipling. I am thinking here, above all, of the physical courage which, even though in a Freudian key, constitutes for Hemingway, as previously it did for Kipling, the greatest virtue of the white man. In Africa this type of courage tends, today, to be supplanted by other more necessary qualities. For courage there will always be a need, perhaps even more so than in the past; but it will no longer be the courage of the hunter Wilson in *The Short Happy Life of Francis Macomber* who shoots a lion dead at a distance of two paces; it will be a different courage, less picturesque, more civilized and, above all, no longer the exclusive quality of the white man but of all those who, whether white or black, are

25

exerting themselves during these years to transform the face of Africa.

In the meantime, however, Hemingway comes irresistibly back into one's mind as soon as one arrives at certain places in East Africa. It must be admitted that the places which bring Hemingway to mind are among the most beautiful in the Black Continent. I am thinking of the so-called game reserves or natural parks in which safaris take place, that is, the shooting expeditions for big game for the benefit of rich Europeans in search of sensation. Hemingway, in his African stories, has described more than one safari; and in a way the safari spirit, a spirit more or less characteristic of tourists and snobs and by no means devoid of vulgarity and unconscious evil, is the limit of his whole African experience.

In Swahili, which is the lingua franca of East Africa, safari means 'journey'. In this original sense, I too have gone on safari. One fine morning, in fact, I left the island of Zanzibar and in stages, by aeroplane, made my way to Arusha, on the lower slopes of the majestic Mount Meru. At Arusha, a Swiss-type village clambering up to the edge of the forest, I found the provision lorry from a motel about a hundred kilometres away, which, bumping along over bad roads and tracks, transported me across the steppe-like upland plain to Lake Manyara.

I went to bed in the unquiet darkness of the African night; the motel, dark as it was, appeared to me to have its rooms arranged in a circle round an abyss that shone like silver in the silent, misty light of a full moon. Next morning I left my room and, in the already burning sunshine, took my way by instinct along a path through acacia trees. The path led towards a low wall, beyond which there seemed to be nothing but emptiness. Having reached the wall, I stood still and looked down.

Before me stretched an immense panorama, typically African, in other words prehistoric; a panorama of a kind, that is, to suggest as though by enchantment the presence of the vanished monsters of the various geological ages, dinosaurs, mammoths, flying dragons. A steel-grey, smooth lake, illuminated here and there by confused, blinding flashes of light, stretched away to the limits of the horizon; mountains in the shape of tables or statueless pedestals encircled it on all sides. The slopes of these mountains, black with forests, fell vertically to the shore of the lake, which was very wide and flat and of a livid whiteness thinly infiltrated by beds of reeds. The dense mountains, the metallic waters, the marshy shore, even the sky with its high, motionless clouds – all these gave the impression of a world still mute and destitute of human voices and presences, of a limitless stage upon which the only actors were the plants and the animals.

Then I lowered my eyes. Two hundred metres farther down the forest seethed, like a kind of green liquid detergent at perpetual boiling-point. This was the African forest, black, dense, oppressive, teeming, heavy, lustrous. Then, suddenly, I had the impression that the forest was moving.

I looked more carefully and then I understood: it was a herd of elephants, well camouflaged amongst the foliage of the trees, feeding as it moved along the slope of the mountain. Now I recognized the ears like the great leaves in the marshes, the barrel-shaped backs, the stumpy, cylindrical feet, the upward-curling trunks, the little pig-like tails hanging downwards. They browsed as they moved; and they had in them the disconcerting mixture of innocence and power which seems to be a characteristic feature of nature's monsters. They had a look of remoteness down there in the depth of the forest, at a great distance; but was this the distance of space or rather that of the vanished ages from which, almost by a miracle, they had survived?

That same afternoon, in one of those special cars with an opening in the roof, which are used for big game hunting, I went down to the lake. After driving through the forest which I had seen from above, we at last came out into the plain. There was the tall grass, of a pale, parched green; the big round shrubs; the little twisted acacias. The water of the lake, grey and smooth, sparkled every now and then between one shrub and another. But of lions, leopards and the herbivorous creatures which are their prey – zebras, gazelles, large antelopes, wart-hogs – there were none. There was no sign, either, of the buffaloes and rhinoceroses that normally live in such places. The plain appeared empty as far as the eye could see, in a quiet, yellow, sickly light, like an old, faded daguerreotype.

I told the driver, a young Negro with a diligent, prudent expression, to go towards the part of the reserve where the wild animals could be seen. Smilingly he replied that we were already in that part of the reserve. At the same time the car came to a stop.

I stood up on the seat and looked out of the opening in the roof. A hot, sluggish wind was blowing, in which it seemed to me that I was aware of the smell of Africa, that smell which, slight though it is, is sour, and which seems to exclude all purity. The sun was blazing, motionless, on the shrubs, the acacias, the lake. Then, in the long grass, something moved and suddenly the enormous tawny head of a lion came into view among the thin, green stalks. The lion rose to its feet, looking in the direction of the lake, then it silently opened its mouth, contracting its lips and displaying its large white canine teeth. It looked as though it wished to get its breath and accumulate the fury required to give its voice the proper tone of menace.

And in fact, a moment later, came the roar, bursting forth in the form of a deep, cavernous rumbling. It was now standing up, its body, which looked slender and small in comparison with its head, stretching forward with all the muscles showing beneath the skin and its long tail, ending in a dark tuft, lowered towards the ground. Summoned by the roar, a lioness which I had not seen rose slowly out of the grass, placing her smooth round head behind that of the male. The roaring finally ceased; and the two lions moved forward slowly and lazily, as though bored and disgusted but determined to take no notice of us. They went past at ten paces' distance to another shrub, and at once lay down amongst the tall grass, disappearing completely. I looked, but now again there was nothing to be seen. I knew, however, that the lions were there, that they were lying there and could see me although I could not see them and could not even point to the spot where they were.

The car started off again and we came out on to the shore of the lake. Have you ever seen those surrealist pictures with vertiginous perspectives of open plains dotted here and there with brilliant, precise objects? The lake shore was like that. White, with a foul, dirty whiteness, it looked as if it were besprinkled, as far as the eye could reach, with what appeared to be fragments of skeletons, of bones and skulls. We drove close to one of these heaps of bones and then I discovered that it was the trunk of a tree with a few branches, skeleton-like, white, corroded by sun and sand.

It was lying there like the skeleton of a man who had died of hunger and thirst in that deserted place, and one realized that it must have fallen of its own accord, from old age, and must have been transported there by the wind or by the lake being flooded, and then left to glisten in the sun. This too was a characteristic feature of Africa: trees in Africa die of old age, they fall and disintegrate, and all this without any intervention from man because there is no man to intervene.

As we drove on, I saw another of these shining, skeleton-like trees; but when we drew close to it, I discovered to my surprise that this was actually the skeleton of an animal, a buffalo probably, judging at least by the enormous black horns projecting from the skull, which was smothered by sand, and by the great arched vertebrae sticking up amongst the stones. Devoured by lions, dead from old age – who could tell? Thus on this shore there was revealed another characteristic of nature when man is absent: death undisturbed, left to itself, side by side with life. Man himself does not allow death to be present side by side with life. Cemeteries, rubbish carts, suburban sites used as refuse dumps: man carefully obliterates all traces of death, pretending to himself that he lives in a world in which there is only life.

We went forward for another half-kilometre along the skeleton-strewn shore, and then, all of a sudden, as we came round a bend, the game reserve became populated. In front of us, right on the edge of the lake, some great ostriches fled away, their bundles of black feathers oscillating below their long necks; farther on, a herd of zebra, big, fat and sleek, streaked the distant air with their white and black stripes; farther still, countless numbers of yellow and black gazelles darted – one might almost say spurted – away through the grass, in the direction of the plain; and finally, in the far distance, a long row of buffaloes, with their thin legs and huge bodies, was moving away, black and monumental against the misty background of the prairie. Other smaller animals appeared amongst the shrubs, foxes, possibly, or warthogs or dwarf antelopes. The reserve seemed to be filled with life; and it was an astonishing thing that the lions and the herbivorous beasts, that is, those which eat and those which are eaten, should be living close together, unaware of each other and as though in happy harmony.

I was standing up, as I said, on the seat of the car; and several times, perhaps because the place suggested it, I imagined myself to be actually a Hemingway character, to have a gun in my hands and to be aiming at a buffalo or a lion or else a gazelle or a zebra. But I realized that, however much I tried to enter into the part of a hunter, I did not succeed in divesting myself of the very precise feeling that killing one of these animals would be a murder neither more nor less than killing a man. Then in the end I seemed to understand. In order to be a hunter one must put oneself, so to speak, into the shoes of a man of today. We live in a time of 'consumer civilization', and elephants and lions, for hunters on safari, are, fundamentally, like cars and refrigerators: objects that are 'consumed', that is, destroyed, to give way to others which are better or cheaper. It was simply that I was not managing to be up-to-date, contemporaneous. In other words, I had not succeeded in forgetting that, whereas cars and refrigerators can be replaced with the greatest ease, lions and elephants, once they are 'consumed', disappear for ever.

6

The Paradise that was an Inferno

Zanzibar, May 1963

Zanzibar is a place that it would be difficult not to describe as enchanting. Imagine a thick grove of coconut-palms covering a good part of the island; and nothing is more elegant, more mysterious, more fairy-like – with the possible exception of a pine forest – than a grove of palms, with their slim, bare trunks of light brown, never vertical but leaning this way and that, in a criss-cross, interlacing perspective which is complicated and redoubled by the indirect reflections of sunlight filtering through the high foliage. Underneath the palm-trees it is empty and this emptiness, as far as the eye can reach, is steeped in a green and golden light in which everything shines and flourishes, even to the last blade of grass. Large huts, with roofs of drooping straw, nestle among the palms, in front of small open spaces in which are piled-up pyramids of coconuts; and they give the impression, whether wrongly or not, of a lazy, pleasant, dreamy, happy existence. When there are no palm-groves, cultivated areas of thick light-coloured shrubs display an intense green in the sunshine; from them comes a sweet, familiar smell reminiscent of bakers' shops in the morning when they are making the cakes for the day: this is from cloves, of which Zanzibar is the biggest exporter in the world.

The coast of Zanzibar, moreover, conveys the feeling of an earthly paradise more than any other place in the world, except possibly the great beaches of Brazil. In the little bays the water, of a luminous transparency, is an intense green, streaked and smooth and glittering, at the same time both dazzling and placid; the sand is as white as snow, and big pink crabs run over this shining sand, and in it are stuck black, rotten pieces of jetsam that make one think of ancient shipwrecks. The palms bend over the beach, thin and tortuous, their dishevelled leaves bright in the sun; long, narrow boats, hollowed out by fire from the trunk of a single tree, lie on the shore; the sea makes a gentle sound like silk as it withdraws and then throws itself upon the white, clean rocks amongst which are scattered little red branches of coral and massive yellow shells that look like small marble ears.

In Zanzibar, the little Arab town has all the characteristics of a decorous, harmonious, honest civilization even though now decayed and melancholy. The narrow, tortuous lanes which the sun penetrates with difficulty are flanked by tall houses which have, on their top floors, galleries shut away behind closely perforated wooden gratings. The four-leafed windows are made in such a way that you can partly open them and look into the street without being seen. On the ground floor level the big doors, justly famous, are of heavy, massive African wood richly and charmingly carved in geometrical or floral designs, and have great bronze locks and handles, elaborate and covered with arabesques. The entire Arab quarter, with its winding lanes and irregular broader openings, slopes down to the gardens that lie between the sea and the Sultan's palace. This last is a building in Indian style, very fine and giving a feeling of lightness and coolness because it is surrounded, on every floor, by big open galleries with fluttering awnings. In the daytime it is extremely hot and the Arab town is plunged in silence and sleep; but as soon as twilight comes, the municipal gardens are filled with people, since this is the time when a delicious breeze comes blowing in from the ocean. Arabs, Indians and Africans throng the gardens fronting the vast expanse of sea on which the lights of a few ships at anchor are already shining. The children chase each other, the women walk in groups holding one another by the hand, numbers of people collect round the barrows where, by the blinding light of acetylene flares, you can gulp down a large glass of sugar-cane squash or eat some tropical fruit that tastes so sweet as to be nauseating.

And yet this paradise, once upon a time, was an inferno, in the most literal sense of the word; and the merchants of the Arab town whom, after visiting their quarter, so attractive and so humane, we readily imagine to have been venerable and serene, with long white beards, immaculate garments and a language elegantly adorned with verses from the Koran – these same merchants lived and prospered by means of the most horrifying traffic there has ever been in the world: the slave-trade. For centuries Zanzibar was the greatest slave-market in this part of the world. The seductive melancholy, the civilized decay of Zanzibar are the melancholy and decay produced by the abolition of the slave-trade in 1897. Thus it was that the seasoned, poetical beauty of the Arab quarter was, if expressed in Marxist terminology, the superstructure of an economic structure founded upon the trade in human flesh. One is sorry to say so, but this is one of those cases in which money gained by inhuman cruelty and insensibility does not seem to have produced, as we say today, any alienation, that is, any unreality, of a corrupt and vulgar kind.

The slave-trade was carried on by cruel methods which perhaps it is opportune to recall. The Negroes, rounded up in their peaceful villages in the centre of Africa by the Arab merchants already mentioned, were made to march on foot over the murderous trails, chained like wild animals. But once they had arrived in Zanzibar they were washed and cleaned up, rubbed with perfumed oil and adorned, according to age and sex, with pieces of material, gold and silver necklaces, feathers and turbans. Thus beautified and attired, they were drawn up in a column and the merchant placed himself at the head of the column which filed through the streets of Zanzibar in the direction of the market-place. As they went on their way, the merchant, in a loud voice, would extol the qualities of his human merchandise; and the little procession would halt each time a purchaser asked to examine, point by point, one of the slaves. The examination was in every way similar to that to which a horse or a mule is subjected before being bought: the prospective buyer would feel the leg and arm muscles, would scrutinize without any shame the most intimate parts of the body, would look into the mouth to see if the teeth were sound, would make the slave run and jump and dance, would inquire whether he had any diseases or whether he snored in his sleep. As soon as the buyer made up his mind, the slave would immediately be stripped of all his adornments and handed over to his new master, who would drag him away on a rope, like a beast of burden. The other slaves, once they had reached the market-place, would be exhibited on a platform and sold off gradually, one after another. The slave, of course, was a mere piece of property; and no account was taken either of age, or of family ties, or of sex, or of any consideration other than his commercial value. Once sold, he was treated as a domestic animal, that is, either well or badly but always without any human regard, according to his master's inclination.

Slavery is one of the mysteries of Africa, all the more obscure inasmuch as it is best known under its historical aspects. The economic reason, as usual, explains nothing: slavery, even more than an economic fact, is a human fact, that is, psychological and in a wide sense religious and cultural. The mystery of slavery is twofold: it must be considered from the point of view of the slave-owners and from the point of view of the slaves. With regard to the slave-owners, all we need to point out is that they were cruel, insensitive and avaricious because they believed, in all good faith, that their own culture was the only culture possible, and seeing that the culture of the Negroes was different from theirs they concluded that the Negroes were not men but beasts. In other words, the slave-owner was a racialist of a very modern type; in the name of culture, he denied the slave humanity, that is, brotherhood; from there, it was only a step to treating the Negro as merchandise. But what else, in recent years, did the Nazis do with the peoples of Eastern Europe?

With regard to the slaves, however, one cannot help wondering what share of responsibility the Africans themselves had in this tragedy of the slave-trade. We are forced to admit that certain historical characteristics of African culture have certainly favoured slavery. In the first place it is known that the Arab and European slave-dealers found an active collaboration among the kings and tribal chiefs of the whole of Black Africa. These monarchs considered their subjects not as citizens (even if strictly limited in their individual freedoms) but as pieces of property, neither more nor less. So it seemed perfectly natural to barter them for the beads, the brass and copper wire, the materials and the firearms of the slave-dealers. In the beginning, it seems, the Negro kings handed over to the slave-dealers only those of their subjects who had committed some crime or other; but afterwards it became common usage to round up and carry off entire innocent populations. In other words, the slave-dealers did very much what the big game hunters on safari do today; they paid a price for the right to seize so many young girls, so many women with children, so many boys, so many adult men. It is understandable that, having seen the chiefs accept the metamorphosis of their own subjects into merchandise, they had no scruples later on about selling this same merchandise, or allowing it to perish or actually destroying it.

A word remains to be said about cannibalism, which was frequent in Africa two centuries ago and which, in our opinion, is connected with the slavery of that time and of all time. Cannibalism was almost always a matter of ritual and magic; but on the slave-dealers it was bound to have the effect of being, on the other hand, purely economic, due, that is, to the chronic food scarcity of Africa. The slave-dealers were wholly ignorant of the magic that was at the source of cannibalism; and they could not but observe that the man who serves as food for another man has all the characteristics of a mere object, and is, in fact, an object *par excellence* inasmuch as he is completely and immediately utilized by means of mastication, swallowing, digestion and defecation. And so it was precisely magic – which according to African intention should serve, through ritual canni- balism, to confirm man's superiority in face of nature, that is, in face of mere objects – it was precisely magic which, contrariwise, by an almost ironical misunderstanding, encouraged the slave-dealers to treat the Negroes as inanimate things.

But when all is said and done, slavery still remains a mystery, just as absolute evil, total defeat (Sartre's *échec total*) are a mystery. This sordid, sinister mystery throws its cold shadow over the warm, languid beauties of Zanzibar and causes them to feel like so many screens provided by an altogether too complacent nature to conceal an atrocious reality. Today, in the place where the slave-market was once held, there is an ugly Protestant church and a luxuriantly green public garden. But anyone who wanders round the aisles of the church or lingers in the shade of the great trees with their flaming red flowers, cannot but reflect that an ugly Christian shrine and a fine tropical garden may perhaps suffice to wipe out the memory of past slavery but not to prevent the possibility of slavery in the future. Slavery cannot be ignored by placing a historical label upon it; it must, instead, be considered as a permanent, insidious temptation in all cultures, even the highest and most progressive, as has been seen, alas, in recent times, in the case of German Nazism and Russian Stalinism. And, as a temptation, it must be interpreted and clarified thoroughly, not merely repressed without troubling to track down its profound sources.

7

The Abyss of the Centuries

Nairobi, June 1963

Scattered irregularly over the open space there are trees of a dull, faded green. The long, low houses, of only a single floor, do not succeed in completely enclosing the rectangle of trampled, dusty earth. Behind the houses rise the hills, and they too are long and low and of pale green dappled here and there with acacia trees and their shadows.

The houses, for the most part, are occupied by shops with signboards in the English style, with white or yellow letters on a dark background; thus the function of the locality is made clear, as a little emporium for the tribes of the neighbourhood, chiefly for the Masai and the Samburu who are pastoral people and do not cultivate the soil. Looking all round, I saw that not a single type of shop was lacking: ironmongery, textiles, foodstuffs, manufactured goods, tools and so on. All these shops had an Indian look about them, the indescribable look of staleness and squalor and decrepitude that is noticeable in the bazaars of Bombay or Hyderabad. They were dark, with their merchandise spilling out of their doorways, and with the dark face of the Indian shopkeeper and his clean white garment behind the counter.

I needed some corned beef, which is indispensable on a car journey through these solitudes, so I went into a shop which was larger than the others and seemed to summarize them all, a kind of drug-store in the American manner. It was really a very fine shop, especially if one considered that we were at Maralal which is the last place reached by the asphalt road, before the tracks leading to Lake Rudolph. On either side of the door rose pyramids of tinned foods with many-coloured labels, on which were to be seen a salmon leaping from the waters of a Canadian river or an ox standing in the middle of an Australian meadow.

The shelves inside appeared to be piled up with more tinned foods. From the ceiling hung coat-hangers with workmen's blouses and trousers and feminine garments. Heaped up in the corners were spades, ploughshares, fishing-rods, umbrellas and brooms. As I leant on the counter I looked up at a shelf, and there was a stuffed crocodile, brown and yellow, glossy as though made of glass and looking as if it were running along the wall, its wide-open mouth bristling with teeth. I asked the young Indian assistant for some corned beef: he had huge, black, bilious-looking eyes, a very low forehead and no chin, a big nose hanging down over a weak mouth, long smooth hair parted at one side. Suddenly I became conscious of the presence of someone at my side. This person was not touching me but I could feel there was somebody there. Then I turned.

It was a young woman of perhaps twenty years old. Her head, small and round, and her hair, arranged in a number of long, quite distinct, closely knotted little plaits, was reminiscent of the sculptures of Benin, and had the precision of a work of art combined with the rusty colour and the rough quality of iron. These little plaits formed ridges over the whole of the top of her head, but at the back they disappeared beneath a cap made of dried cow dung. Her face did not have the prognathous quality that is so striking in the Negroes of Guinea: her eyes were set level with the surface of her face but not protuberant; her nose flat and dilated but not snub; her lips big and fleshy but not projecting. She had a very long neck, but I judged this not so much from the neck itself which was not visible as from the iron-mongery that encircled it. Circles and circles of some dark metal, possibly copper, started at the top of her throat, grew tighter round her neck and then widened out again so as to form a kind of metal bib covering her shoulders and and the top part of her chest. Her ears caught my attention: the lobes had been pierced and the hole enlarged until the lobe itself had become nothing more than a little frame of flesh round the huge cork plug inserted into it, of the kind usually to be seen on the largest wine-barrels. From this plug hung a small necklace of blue and red beads. Another similar necklace lay on top of the bib of copper rings. I looked at her body: she wore a short dark-red tunic glued, as it were, to her powerful form; her legs and feet were bare. At her wrists and ankles were more copper rings, great numbers of them, reaching to her knees and elbows.

Beside her stood a young man completely naked except for a little red rag stretched round his hips. Half of his face and half of his chest were painted red; and also behind, half of his back down to his loins. On his head were the same little plaits as the woman's, but falling down on to his forehead; and the same cow-dung cap. He did not lean against the counter as the woman did, who seemed to be pretending that she wanted to buy something whereas in reality it was quite obvious that she had come in out of idle curiosity: he remained standing in the middle of the shop, leaning with an air of indifference on a long iron-pointed spear. In his hand he clasped a stick which ended in a big, massive knob.

As I looked at them I had the same feeling as is aroused by a uniform or a ceremonial costume or any other kind of dress of undoubted symbolical significance – an almost scientific curiosity, as though I were faced with an obscure message that had to be deciphered. But European military uniforms and ceremonial costumes are easily related to a well-known, familiar culture; whereas these copper rings, this red paint, these plaits and cow-dung caps were the product of a wholly foreign culture, expressive, probably, of a still direct and uninterrupted relationship with nature. This is as much as to say that this man and woman were, for me, as it were, masked, whereas in reality they were merely indecipherable. In other words, between them and me there was an abyss of ten or fifteen thousand years; and how could this gap be closed?

The Indian handed me the tin of corned beef; I paid, left the shop and went and got into the car to wait for my companions who had gone away. There, as I looked round the open space, which meanwhile had become peopled with other figures like those I had seen in the drug-store, I continued with my reflections. Was it then possible to have any relationship with a woman dressed in copper rings and a man painted red, when one had arrived two days before in a jet plane from a city such as New York or Paris? And was it not significant that the possibility of such relations was occurring at this particular moment, at a time when, in the so-called Western world, human relations are reduced to an exchange of commonplaces and slogans, to an automatism of conventions, to the free play of few instincts? That is to say, was it not significant, perhaps, that magical and naturalistic prehistory should be coming to the surface with the Africans and the primitive peoples of the whole world at a moment when the history of the Europeans is at a crisis?

Relations with the Africans, of course, remain nevertheless very difficult, even though history, as in the past, no longer interposes itself between us and them. I remember in this connection an Italian missionary in Kenya who confessed to me that, after ten years of residence and of preaching in a wild locality on the borders of the Sudan, he had succeeded in making only one convert. I remember the bare, humble room in the Mission, the unpainted wooden furniture, the picture of the Pope and that of a Negro bishop, the embroidered table-cloth and the vase of flowers on top of the cloth, the Nuremberg cuckoo-clock, the modest, hard divan and chairs; and I say to myself that this single convert proved nothing either against the Africans or against the Christian religion. It showed, if anything, the enormous difficulty, for the African, of leaping an abyss of thousands of years, as is proposed to him by the whites. And in order to find himself, paradoxically, in a world full of irrational fears and naturalistic myths that are, basically, not so very different from his own.

But there remains in my memory the glance of the girl dressed in copper rings, a glance of bashful, shy humanity; like a modest appeal to a remote, archaic brotherhood.

Two days later I had, by chance, a confirmation of my reflections. We were driving through a region that seemed more dreamlike than real, an immense plain of a colourless,

40

misty green, dotted in the far distance with mysterious herds of wild animals; and here and there, as far as the eye could reach, were scattered acacias with umbrella-like foliage and red ant-hills like warts. All of a sudden I caught sight of something round showing white in the sun, not very far from the road, and I told the driver to stop. The car came to a halt; as I had imagined, this was a group of huts of the Samburu tribe.

We walked through the tall, pale grass which divided as we passed. There was a profound silence, in which the only sound was the whirring of the cinema camera with which one of our party was filming the landscape.

There was a fence, or rather, a confused tangle of brambles round the open space. We passed through an opening that was perhaps a gate, and found ourselves in a space which was trampled all over and full of animals' footprints. Round us stood three huts.

At first sight these huts looked like three enormous chrysalises from which the caterpillar, transformed into a butterfly, had flown away. Or three enormous white worms. The white colour is that of the dried cow-dung with which they are covered. The dung forms a strange surface like large sheets of armour plating, with cracks zig-zagging here and there.

I was surprised at the lowness of the entrance openings. Stooping down, not without a shudder since the huts appeared to be abandoned and might have become the refuge of some reptile or wild animal, I crept through the aperture. Bent double, I crawled through a kind of corridor a couple of metres long and then came out into the dwelling-place itself. Thus the hut was made like a snail's shell, or like a certain type of bird's nest to be found in Africa on baobab trees, having the shape of a shoe: a very low entrance, a very narrow passage and then the room, so that any sort of wild beast trying to come in could be easily driven back from inside.

Gradually, in the half-darkness, I distinguished signs that the builders of this lair were undoubtedly human: four stones, smokestained and scorched, round a little heap of ashes and a few black, dead embers, in other words, the hearth; a little peep-hole, from which a small amount of light filtered, in other words, a window; and, behind a partition, a framework of reeds on the floor, in other words, a bed.

It was impossible to stand upright inside the hut; anyone living there would have to resign himself to a life of squatting beside the hearth or lying on the bed. What struck me most was the lowness of the ceiling. Why so low? From an unconscious imitation, possibly, of the den in which animals huddle to sleep or devour their prey. It is the animals, therefore, which have taught the Samburu how to build themselves a house; and the Samburu, pupils without much independence of their own, have merely added a very few indispensable innovations – the stones so as to light a fire, of which the animals have no need because they do not cook their food; the little window, which the animals can do without because they are day-blind; the pallet of reeds which is of no use to the animals because they sleep on the ground, inside their own skins. A very few innovations; but enough to bear witness that the inhabitants were human and to arouse a sense of identification in us.

And so, indeed, it was: visiting a wild beast's lair it does not occur to us to put ourselves in the place of a lion or a fox; but visiting a Samburu hut, though it is so like a wild beast's lair except for those three small innovations I have mentioned, I could not help thinking: here am I squatting, naked, painted red, dressed in copper rings, together with my wife who is also naked and adorned with copper rings, in this den; here am I, and I have gone back twenty thousand years; and this is my home. And now, after devouring a piece of raw meat or some millet gruel, I shall lie down on the pallet of reeds, I shall listen for a short time to the silence of the African night and then I shall go to sleep. And tomorrow I shall get up at dawn, leave the hut and drive my sheep out of the enclosure towards the dangerous grassland that is visited by lions and leopards. In one hand I shall have my club, in the other my spear; and my body will be half painted red. And it will be a day like all other days, from twenty thousand years ago onwards.

42

8

The Kikuyu Schoolmaster

Nairobi, June 1963

We drove round for some time from one country road to another – roads of red earth like newly butchered meat, shaded by trees of rich, dark green, under a cloudless sky whose dazzling blue was reminiscent of the enamelled pans in old-fashioned kitchens. Finally we saw some boys of about fifteen, probably students, all of them in white short-sleeved shirts, white shorts and orange ties. We stopped two of them and asked where the school was. Their faces, alert and as though anxious to please us, lit up with broad white smiles. They pointed out the direction with repeated gestures and many explanations in a sing-song, childish but correct English.

There, in fact, was the school, and the usual blood-coloured soil, cultivated with only moderate success to resemble an English lawn; and, round the lawn, various buildings of unplastered brick, long and low and on only one floor: the refectory, the classrooms, the chapel, the headmaster's quarters, the dormitories. It was the usual plan of an Anglo–Saxon school; there were even coloured posts on the lawn to act as goal-posts for football; but everything was on a smaller, poorer, more restricted, more modest scale than at a similar place in England or the United States. On the other hand, moreover, it cannot be denied that the school had the look of a serious, reliable establishment. One had the feeling, in fact, that within certain rather narrow financial limits this school had not been built merely to throw dust in people's eyes, but rather for the real education and instruction of the young Kikuyu.

After a short time the headmaster, followed by two of the

teachers, came to meet us. It would be difficult to imagine, from the physical point of view at any rate, a more British type of man – red hair *en brosse*, red toothbrush moustache, a freckled white face and, in the midst of all the freckles, small, very blue eyes. A rather shy, certainly bashful expression was partly contradicted by the big, authoritative pipe that he held between his teeth. He was wearing a very loose, short-sleeved shirt, khaki shorts, woollen stockings up to his knees and large, well-polished shoes with triple soles. He greeted us affably but with a kind of almost diffident detachment; he introduced the two teachers, one of them tall, fair and phlegmatic, the other dark, small and nervous; then placed himself at the head of the group for a tour of the school.

The first impression of poverty and seriousness was confirmed. In the dormitories, for instance, there were two rows of camp-beds with slate-grey woollen blankets, and the boys' boxes or fibre suitcases were on the floor beside them. There were walls of unplastered brick and a grey cement floor. The chapel was a sort of barn with benches of raw wood, a small brand-new organ on which two boys were at that moment practising, and a high ceiling like that of a Polynesian hut, with beams and tiles. In a classroom we saw blackish benches in three rows, the teacher's desk of light-coloured wood, a chair, a blackboard, a map. Then the kitchen, a big room where the potato soup for supper was boiling in a number of cauldrons on the stoves. And finally the library: four shelves, tired-looking books, odd and irregular.

Afterwards, when we had completed our tour, the head-master invited us for tea in his private quarters. We sat in a comfortable little sitting-room; through the wide-open windows there was a view over the green and red hills surrounding the school. And then, sitting in a deep, flower-patterned armchair, a cup of tea on one knee and a plate with a slice of apple-pie on the other, I embarked at once on my main question. I said that the school, with its bare, dignified and rather bloodless poverty, reminded me of the Catholic and Protestant missions in Africa. There too, as here, was a great ambition, a great purpose. Here, it was to graft the Africans into Western culture, there, to convert them to the Christian religion. And at the same time, here as there, there were limited means, poverty, unpretentiousness, a look of simplicity and cheerlessness. But in Europe the churches, for centuries, have kindled the imagination of the faithful with artistic splendour, with the magnificence of their furnishings; and the universities are installed in stately, solemn, severe buildings. But where could one find richness, artistic display, stateliness and solemnity in the buildings constructed by Europeans in Africa? Certainly not, as one could see, in the missions and the schools, humble and cheerless as they were; but rather in the banks and the commercial headquarters with their proud polished marble and massive doors; in the neo-capitalist hotels, among the most luxurious in the world; in the shops overflowing with manufactured goods; in the cafés, restaurants and night-clubs, all of them attractive, ornate and original. Was it not to be wondered at, then, that the Africans, seeing that for Europeans culture and religion take second place in relation to trade, money, satisfaction of the senses and luxury – was it not to be wondered at, I asked, that they do not become converted nor allow themselves to be instructed to the degree that would be desirable, and that they think that Western civilization is predominantly hedonistic and mercantile and above all, basing themselves upon this idea, that they react against Europeans in the way we have seen in recent years almost everywhere in Africa?

The headmaster listened to me, smoking his pipe and grasping it between two fingers as though ready to take it out from between his teeth and answer me. But, when I fell silent, he took quite a long time before he spoke. He coughed slightly, cleared his throat, coughed again, then, uttering his words with difficulty and from time to time almost stammering, he said that recently some dignified universities had been built in Africa; and that anyhow he was exceedingly satisfied with his African pupils.

In general, he added, turning aside from my question,

the Kikuyu schoolboys were much more diligent, more studious and more serious than the British schoolboys whom he had taught for many years. The reason was that the Kikuyu boys were conscious of the fact that receiving an education now constituted a privilege and a piece of good fortune in Kenya and so they made an effort to show themselves worthy of this extraordinary distinction. British boys, on the other hand, consider it an obvious and undisputed right and consequently do not work at their studies. He concluded, after a final fit of coughing, that it was to be doubted whether the Kikuyu boys would acquire a real mastery of English culture: for the moment, it was memory rather than understanding which activated them. In other words, they learn by heart everything that they do not understand. But learning by heart was nevertheless preferable to not studying at all, as too often happens in English schools.

And how about the future? What would become of these schools after Kenya had become independent? The headmaster recognized that the future was a little uncertain, at any rate with regard to his own personal position. He would be able to remain at the school, but he would no longer be headmaster; in his place there would be a Kikuyu teacher to whom he would have to be subordinate. This was a reason for his thinking it would be better for him to go back to England and there resume his not very successful teaching of the lazy British boys.

And how about European culture? What would happen to European culture, after independence? The headmaster did not seem to understand, or at best he understood only partially. Slowly he said that, for the moment at least, the teaching of the English language and literature would continue; that the Kikuyu, as indeed a great many other peoples in Africa, needed a European language in order to express certain things and above all to be on terms of understanding with other African peoples; and that anyhow the schools would be in good hands inasmuch as the Kikuyu were not only very good pupils but also good teachers. He went on in this vein for some time, praising the Kikuyu and expressing confidence for the future. And I myself, recognizing in him an evasiveness and reticence under a mask of empirical optimism, finally let the subject drop.

I had the answer to my question a few days later, while I was travelling through the northern part of Kenya, from one village to another. We found ourselves on a big European estate, with a villa occupied by the owner, a stud-farm, the cultivation of early fruit, a garden, a swimming-pool and so on. After all these luxuries, I asked to see the school of a Kikuyu village situated on the estate. My request was immediately granted: the school was only a few steps from the villa, we could go there on foot, it was only a short walk.

I remember the situation of the school as one of the most typically African landscapes I ever happened to see during my journey: a lake whose waters were motionless and pale as silver, full of inlets and meanderings among small, smoky mountains of the usual truncated conical shape so common in Africa; a meadow surrounded by trees like those of the Garden of Eden in carved Romanesque bas-reliefs – thick, smooth trunks and a tuft of a few large leaves; some hermetic huts with drooping roofs of blackened straw. As twilight fell the sky was almost green, with a few white, glittering stars, and the silence was frightening like that of a prehistory populated by monsters. Indeed I should not have been surprised to see the huge body, the long neck, the minute head of a dinosaur appear between one hill and the next, against the background of the lake.

Instead of this, however, there emerged, all of a sudden, from one of the huts, the schoolmaster. He was a young Kikuyu, sturdy and rustic-looking, with a face at the same time both crude and intense in its expression. There was a hint of delusion and of ingenuousness in the bold glance of his eye, in his frequent bursts of laughter, in the way in which he stood with legs wide apart, almost pugnaciously, in the middle of the field, amongst the huts in which he lived and taught. He welcomed us cordially, and as soon as he knew that we were journalists and writers almost

47

displayed enthusiasm. His eyes shone, he barely replied to our questions and finally started enumerating the books he had read or of which he had heard: Aristotle, Plato, Homer . . . Shakespeare, Cervantes, Goethe . . . Dante, Tolstoy, Spinoza, Racine . . . At first, at these names, he added some opinion or other, but I could not make out if it was his own or if he had read it in some scholastic work; in the end all he did was to utter the names anyhow, all higgledy-piggledy, as though they were the names of streets or places. It was a kind of cultural landscape that he was describing, the customary landscape of European culture; but to him it evidently seemed wonderful and full of mystery, just as the African landscape which I had before my eyes at that moment seemed to me. And seeing him so solitary, so small and so enthusiastic in the midst of the solemn, gloomy African scenery, I could not help thinking that, after all, the headmaster had not been wrong in saying that European culture was in good hands. But not in the entirely practical, professional sense that he had intended to give to his remarks; rather, in an exceptional, mythological, irrational manner. Almost magical, in fact, just as – to give an example – happened with Virgil and Latin culture during the Middle Ages.

9

The Culture that Prevents an Understanding of Others

Mombasa, July 1963

I recall the dining-room of a big hotel in Mombasa: immaculate tablecloths, shining glass and cutlery, air-conditioning, a Viennese orchestra, waiters in white jackets with silk lapels, a buffet table with all the Western titbits, a discreet bustle of conversation and of dishes. At a table not very far from ours there were about ten men without a single woman. They were all mature men of between forty and fifty, all of them blond and corpulent, all wearing shorts, or rather, long drawers and white short-sleeved shirts. I took a long look at them with the feeling of mixed attraction and hostility that one has for something which one does not completely understand and for which one does not feel any excess of sympathy; and I had to admit privately that here was a set of almost perfect samples of that human species which I shall call 'homo Victorianus' and which it is now difficult to come across, even in England.

The English today rarely have those big, slightly bandy legs, those monumental thighs, those bellies as tight as drums, those muscular chests and massive napes to their necks, those prominent chins and toothbrush moustaches; for the most part, especially in the ruling class, they are thin, intellectualized, long-limbed, loose-knit, elegant. The fact is that between the Victorian era and the present time there has been a political, economic and social revolution and thence also, let it be said, a physiological revolution. But wherever, as in Kenya, the atmosphere of Victorian imperialism has been partially or wholly preserved, then, promptly, the corresponding physical type reappears.

I am not capable of a very great degree of attention and sensitiveness as far as hearing is concerned; but the friend with whom I was sitting at table can actually listen to a conversation that is taking place at the other end of a room. And so it was, that day. Suddenly I saw him stop eating, and almost, one might say, turn the 'pavilions' of his ears in the direction of the round table where the party of men was seated. In the end I inquired: 'Who are they?'

'Nasty brutes.'

'What d'you mean?'

'Landowners, businessmen, company employees.'

'And what are they talking about?'

'They're talking about the Africans, naturally.'

'And what are they saying?'

'They're saying and they're not saying.'

'But what *are* they saying?'

'They're saying nasty things.'

'What d'you mean?'

He was silent for a short time, listening. Then he explained, continuing nevertheless to keep his ears open. 'How is it possible,' he said, 'to give a detailed account of an English conversation? It's a question of hints, of half-tones, of allusions, of accents. Apart from the words themselves, one would have to interpret the clearings of the throat, the stammerings, the hesitations, the hoarsenesses, the falterings. So I can't give you a full account of what they're saying. I can give you a summary of it.'

'Let's hear your summary.'

He listened a little longer; then he resumed: 'The summary of it is this: the Africans will prove themselves incapable of carrying on the administrative, economic and social machine created by the Europeans in Africa. Once the whites have departed, everything will go to pieces. And this, not so much because the Africans are lacking in certain qualifications that can be acquired with time, as because they are essentially incapable of doing certain things, in other words because they are racially inferior.'

'What arguments do they bring forward to prove that statement?'

'No arguments. They are convinced of it from the start. The whole conversation, in fact, is based on this presupposition, which is tacitly shared by them all.'

'And what else are they saying?'

I saw him prick up his ears again, with a look of malicious delight in his eyes. At last he said: 'They're now talking about someone called Harrison who has divorced his wife in order to marry someone called Maud.'

'That's enough, then, I'm not interested.'

The 'homo Victorianus', of whom at that moment I had about ten samples under my eyes, is still to be found today all over Africa, though more and more rarely as the old-type colonialism is replaced by neo-capitalism. But the racist ideas of this 'homo Victorianus', it must be said, are not based solely on interest, as might be thought. Those ten unpleasant men in short-sleeved shirts and shorts were, fundamentally, the unconscious spokesmen of a precise culture: that of the nationalist, individualist, bourgeois, Protestant type which showed its face in Europe immediately after the Reformation. And it is correct that this is so. The European is always conditioned by his own history; in his relations with peoples of other civilizations he always makes use, consciously or not, of highly complex and delicate cultural instruments that have been forged over the centuries. But the culture of Protestant origin is not the only culture of which the Europeans are the spokesmen in Africa.

I had proof of this a few days later on a very different occasion. We were travelling through the southern part of Kenya and at a certain point the driver suggested that we should make a deviation which, he said, would greatly shorten our journey. At the fork in the road there was, it is true, a placard announcing 'Work in Progress, Road closed'; but he assured us that it was an old placard and that the road work had been completed some time ago. So we turned on to the deviation and started off again.

It was an unmetalled road, of earth as red as blood,

leading across a region that had a strange, fabulous, fantastic appearance: hill after hill as far as the eye could reach, deep valleys between the hills and, scattered here and there, one at a great distance from the other, huge, gigantic, solitary baobab trees. We wandered round the hills for some time, stopping at intervals to contemplate the strange landscape; and then, in the deep silence, the baobab trees scattered here and there seemed, with the disconsolate gestures of their leafless branches, to be really animals and not trees, and one almost expected that they would cry out or rise up on their roots and start walking. Then, at a bend, the road all of a sudden came to an abrupt end. There was the torn side of a brilliantly green hill; there was an open space, bright red, and littered with implements and excavating machines painted yellow and motionless in the sun; and finally, in the nearest valley, there was a small prefabricated house.

We went over to it. Immediately an elderly foreman came out, and with him a younger workman, tall and fair. They were the two caretakers of the worksite; all the other workmen, since it was Sunday, had gone off to the town. The foreman was a Ligurian, the workman Piedmontese. They invited us into the house in which a few makeshift pieces of furniture had been arranged, they offered us something to drink, and we began to talk.

Inevitably, after the first inquiries about the road, about the work that was going on, about their families, we started talking about the Africans. This is a compulsory subject of conversation because, everywhere in Africa, the biggest problem of the Europeans, their greatest preoccupation, is, precisely, the Africans themselves. The Ligurian foreman merely uttered a few laconic remarks, reticent even if unfavourable, accompanied by smiles and headshakings; but the Piedmontese workman was more talkative. Just as though we had been inspectors sent by some imaginary international authority to collect complaints, criticisms and reproaches, he launched out into a long diatribe upon the failings of the African labourers who were working on the site together with the whites. I will not stop to repeat his arguments here; they consisted mainly of common-places, even though apparently confirmed by direct personal experience. The essential point of the workman's remarks was that he found fault with the Africans for conducting themselves in a different way from the way in which they ought to conduct themselves, both on the worksite and outside. Now this ideal conduct was, precisely, the conduct observed by the whites. In other words, the workman was finding fault with the Africans for not behaving like Europeans. After his torrent of accusations he concluded with this phrase, pronounced with profound conviction: 'After all, the chief trouble with these people is their ignorance.'

After a short time we said good-bye to them and drove on again, leaving them to their solitude among the baobab trees. But during our journey my thoughts went back to our meeting and I could not help comparing the words of the Italian workman with those of the group of Englishmen in the hotel at Mombasa. The workman, too, in his judgment upon the Africans, had unconsciously set himself up as the spokesman of a precise culture. That of the Englishmen was the Protestant, nationalist culture; that of the workman, humanistic and Catholic. The Englishmen, in fact, found fault with the Africans, from the racialist point of view, for *being* Africans; whereas the workman found fault with them for *behaving* like Africans. The difference was great: in the first case, as far as the Africans were concerned, there was nothing they could do; in the second they could, if they wished, do something, that is, behave in a different way. And whereas, for the English, the inferiority of the Africans was a question of blood and heredity, for the young work-man, on the other hand, it was 'ignorance'.

Ignorance: with this word the unconscious humanism of the workman was expressed in a complete fashion. 'Ignor-ance' meant: these men are like ourselves, merely they are ignorant, in other words 'they do not know'. Whenever they decide to free themselves from ignorance, there will no longer be any difference between the man born on the desolate shores of wild Lake Rudolph and the one born on the flowery banks of kindly Lake Como. More subtly and more drastically still: if the Africans 'knew', they would no longer *be* Africans; that is, they would no longer be black, they would no longer have prognathic faces or curly hair – which is the humanistic conception taken almost to the verge of a miracle.

Naturally neither the Protestant, nationalist, racist conception, nor the humanist, universalist one is really suited to give us an understanding of the Africans, to allow us to establish a non-fictitious relationship with them. Strange to say, the first conception, which is the one more hostile to the Africans, is also the one that makes use of a greater number of scientific notions; the second is purely moral and religious. What they both have in common is that they are cultural instruments for the achievement of a relationship with peoples who, on the contrary, have no culture in the sense that is given to that word in Europe.

It is true that an African culture exists; but it has no intermediary, intellectualist, rational features; it springs from unchanging biological necessity, not from the ever-changing evolution of history. This discrepancy, radical as it is, between the culture of the Africans and that of the Europeans explains, in my opinion, the difficulty, if not impossibility, of a relationship. The ignorance attributed to the Africans by the Piedmontese workman can anyhow be imputed, also, to the Europeans, in a different sense. The more the latter *know*, the more they will be capable to teach. Thus the ignorance of the Europeans is the prime reason for the ignorance of the Africans.

10

A Memory of the Masai

Nairobi, July 1963

Shirley was an English girl, born and brought up in Kenya,
where her father owned a big farm about a hundred kilometres from Nairobi. Her physical type could not have been
more Nordic, more British; she was tall, thin, loose-limbed,
with hair of an ordinary dull blonde, eyes that were blue
but not beautiful because they had a certain fixed, glassy
look, a small, severe nose, a wide mouth and a square jaw.
Not only had Shirley never seen Europe but she had very
seldom been even to Nairobi; her education had been
carried on, somehow or other, at home. Ignorant and
uncultivated, she had a perfect knowledge of Swahili,
which is the lingua franca of East Africa; as well as of the
Kikuyu dialect. Moreover she possessed the skills that can
be acquired in Africa: she knew how to organize an encampment, how to hunt the most diverse wild animals, from
gazelles to lions, how to direct agricultural work on her
father's estate, how to cook, and even, if required, how to
treat certain tropical diseases.

Shirley drove me along bumpy, sandy tracks in her old
Land-Rover, across the green flat spaces and through the
acacia groves of the great plain, to see a curiosity of the
neighbourhood, a little 'zoo' of wild animals collected by an
ex-professional hunter who hires them out by degrees to
cinematograph firms who make films of hunting expeditions
and other adventures in Africa. Shirley drove with a non-
chalance that seemed to indicate long practice; and as she
drove she talked willingly. Or rather, she answered my
questions. She talked without moving, her profile turned

towards me, looking straight ahead at the track; and so, just because she was not looking at me, I tended to pay more attention to her way of speaking than to her attitudes or the expression of her face. Her words came to me clear and precise, as though I were listening to them on the radio.

Shirley's father had decided to leave Kenya, where life for the Europeans would soon become difficult, and to go back to England. I asked Shirley whether she liked the idea of seeing her country of origin for the first time, and what she thought of doing, and whether she would feel nostalgia for Kenya, and other things of the same kind. She answered me positively, but in an entirely colourless, mechanical way. She said she was quite content to leave, to go to England, to start a new life. She would not feel any nostalgia for Kenya, because recently this country had become too unpleasant for the English. She added that she would be all right in England because she had many relations and many friends there. She spoke, as I have said, listlessly, mechanically, in a plain, bloodless English which, on examination, would no doubt be shown to be composed of ready-made phrases. It was the English of not more than a hundred words, such as is spoken by the middle class. I reflected that I had been unlucky to fall in with somebody who was boring and without interests; and, when I looked at Shirley's very ordinary face, I said to myself that I should have expected it.

But, at a fork in the road, in that boundless green solitude, Shirley found herself in doubt, and stopped. There was a light breeze blowing, which caressed one's ears; the sun of the upland plain shone bright but without burning. Then, all of a sudden, a young African emerged from behind a big bush. He was very tall, almost naked, with half his body painted red, his hair divided up into a hundred little plaits, and he held a long spear in one hand and a club in the other. Shirley leaned out of the window and called to him in Swahili. Then I noticed an abrupt change in her voice and in her face. Her voice had become warm, modulated, shrewd, and full of curious inflections that ranged from shyness to authority; her face became animated, and a strange expression of studied ingenuousness and insinuating sympathy shone in her eyes and was apparent in the smile on her lips. As for the African, he answered Shirley's questions in a slow, hesitating voice; but he too, from the first moment, had, as it were, an expression of recognition and of embarrassed acceptance of an unavoidable relationship. Finally Shirley thanked him and we went on our way.

Encouraged, I dropped the subject of England and asked her questions about her life in Kenya. At once she became animated and began telling me about it. Hers had been an untutored youth; she and her brothers spent the whole day wandering round the countryside with a band of Masai boys of their own age. I asked who were the Masai, although I knew perfectly well, simply to hear her talking, and she replied, in an almost sing-song voice, that they were a tribe of herdsmen living in the northern part of Kenya. Tall, slender, elegant, well-built, tireless in the hunt, the Masai were completely resistant to European civilization. Unlike the Kikuyu, they do not become converted to the religion of the Europeans, they do not dress in the manner of Europeans, they do not accept European habits and customs. The Masai character, added Shirley without my asking, was very likeable: gay, carefree, light-hearted. The Masai were frivolous, vain, careless and childish; they laughed and joked all the time. Shirley remained thoughtful for a moment, looking at the road; then, as though urged by an irresistible need to talk about the Masai, she added that these pastoral people live on blood and milk. They suck the milk straight from their beasts, the blood they also suck in the same way, rather like the milk. In other words, having made an incision in a vein, they drink the blood and then close up the vein again.

I observed a short time ago that Shirley's speech was plain and bloodless, and that in talking she made use of the hundred words that constitute the entire language of her class. But in speaking of the Masai her language, I realized, had changed, as had her voice and her expression. Her speech had become much richer and warmer; and, from what source I know not, words of an almost literary stamp, unusual, anyhow, and at the same time genuine, mingled with her usual outworn, vague phrases. It would seem in fact, that – like Antaeus, son of the Earth, who drew renewed strength every time his feet touched the soil – Shirley's speech regained vigour and colour whenever she spoke of Africa and the Africans. I tried the opposite experiment, leading the conversation to the work that she would be doing in England, the circles that she would be frequenting there, and, abruptly, her speech again became bloodless and mechanical. She now expressed herself in words that had the dryness and aridity of formulas of exchange; her face had become cold and hard again; her eyes were now staring and empty. It would perhaps be too much to say that she had become a different person; if anything, it could be safely asserted that the real Shirley was the one who became warm and animated when speaking of Africa. Only, by a curious contradiction, Shirley rejected her own African nature; she wished to be especially and only English. In fact, even in her liking for the Masai, one could not but notice, in turn, a slight, disdainful note of detachment, mitigated however by an indefinable attraction and curiosity. Indeed there were many complications and subtleties in the relations between Europeans and Africans. And Shirley, involuntarily, furnished a good example of them.

We left the principal track, went through a wooden gate between two fences that vanished into the distance and seemed, in that deserted place, to form the enclosure not so much of a precise, registered property as of a dream, and Shirley, all at once, began speaking warmly again as she recalled her youth in the company of the Masai. They used to go hunting the wart-hog, a kind of wild boar with long tusks projecting from its mouth: the four English children, the Masai and, sometimes, as many as fifteen dogs. And the Masai ran on their long thin legs, brandishing their spears, and they would drive the wart-hogs from their dens and finally kill them. And it was all so exciting, so intense. And the African days were so very, very long, the sun never seemed to go down and every moment of life was new and strange. Shirley was silent for a moment and then, this time again without my asking her, she went on to say that the Masai had no feelings about women, whom they consider to be mere pieces of property. Having no need for affection, all they ask of women is that they should work hard, in the villages, while they, the men, wander over the immense plain, naked and armed like Greek heroes, behind their cows; or else go hunting, another occupation for men alone. Again Shirley was silent, then she told me that a Masai had gone to her father and had asked to buy her – her, Shirley – in order to make her his wife. As she told me this story there was a far-away look in her eye, as though at that moment she saw herself in imagination united by conjugal ties to an African herdsman. But immediately afterwards she concluded by saying, in a hard tone of voice, that the Masai are truly stupid, and that this matrimonial request was yet a further proof of their stupidity.

As we went along the winding path through the tall grass of the plain a group of Masai approached us and more or less barred our passage. They were all armed with spears and clubs, the sun glistened on their ebony foreheads and their eyes were intently fixed upon us. Shirley at once stopped the car and entered upon a long conversation. Again I was struck by the animation, the ambiguity, the singularly familiar tone of her voice and of her expression. Two or three times she smiled; then again she frowned and appeared to be angry. Finally she turned towards me and, abandoning Swahili for English, explained to me that these young men, vain like all the Masai, were asking to be photographed with her. Would I take the photograph?

I accepted willingly. Shirley took a camera out of the locker, explained to me how it worked and then, very nimbly, got out of the car and went to take up her position. The Masai surrounded her, naked, slender, black, unspeakably barbaric and primitive beside her, with their little plaits of hair, their necklaces of coloured beads, their copper bracelets, their red paint which looked like a veil of blood on their black skins. One of them, the tallest and most muscular of them all, put his arm round Shirley's waist, another placed his hand on her shoulder. She hesitated, then smiled broadly and mischievously; in a shrill, clear voice, in which there seemed to be an echo of some kind of pleasure, she called out to me to be careful and set the camera correctly. The Masai, also, were laughing; but Shirley was right: their attitude was, above all, one of vanity and frivolity, and also, it seemed to me, there was a touch of arrogance with regard to Shirley; as though, instead of looking upon her as a person, they considered her to be an object, in other words, in fact, a woman.

The photograph having been taken, Shirley extricated herself unhurriedly from the Masai, got back into the car and, waving her hand in farewell, started off again along the track. We drove on for barely a kilometre, and then the little private zoo, the goal of our expedition, came into view. Two or three large, decrepit, dusty trees provided shade to some huts and a row of cages. As we approached, I saw that the cages had big, heavy bars of dark wood; behind the bars there were glimpses, in the shadows, of the outlines of wild beasts, large and small; a couple of giraffes raised their little inquisitive heads, on the end of long, thick necks, above the cages, from an adjoining enclosure.

The car came to a stop. Shirley jumped out and went to meet the keeper of the zoo, a wiry, grey Englishman who looked like a bank clerk. Their conversation was brief, and its very brevity confirmed my observations: that Shirley, animated, warm and articulate when speaking of the Masai or talking to them, with her compatriots fell back on the worn-out words and automatic quality of behaviour that are part and parcel of social relations in an industrial civilization.

It appeared that the owner of the zoo was away; he had left to accompany a couple of lions that were being used in the making of a film entitled, very appropriately, *African Temptation*. Shirley asked me whether I wanted to look round the zoo; I answered her, in accordance with the tone of her inquiry, that to me it did not matter; and she, relieved, said: 'All these animals in the cages are absolutely uninteresting. In the cages they lose their personality, which depends on spontaneity and freedom. What you need to see is a free lion walking amongst the bushes on the plain; a free elephant standing still, lurking amongst the foliage of the forest; a free rhinoceros as it raises its black head above the yellow grass.'

All this she said as she continued to drive the car in her usual slapdash, carefree manner. Her eyes were wandering over the immensity of the plain, in a strange way, as though she were looking for something. And then, all at once, I could not help picturing her in London or some other English town, in a foggy, gloomy Nordic winter. And I said to myself that, even there, her eyes from time to time would have a look of enchantment when instinctively, amongst the foul industrial murk, they sought the green outline of the hills of Africa, the sunlight on the high plateau, and the small, black, elegant figures of the Masai wandering over the pastures with their cattle.

11

Dedan Kimathi

Nairobi, August 1963

Mount Kenya, called by the Kikuyu 'Kera Nyaga' which means 'mountain of splendour', was now in front of me. It is a typical African mountain, that is, at the same time majestic and obscurely menacing. Its immense cone rises from the high plateau with an incline which is by no means precipitous, which is, in fact, so gentle and gradual that its slopes seem to extend, like colossal roots, right to the limits of the horizon. Mount Kenya is entirely covered with a very thick, fur-like forest, of a green that is almost black. The forest reaches up to just below the summit, which is small and bare, faceted and sparkling like a diamond. The mountain looks like a man with a cloak pulled up right under his nose, a man crouching and staring: at any moment he might rise to his feet, stretch out two immense arms and seize hold of the sky and the earth.

According to Kikuyu mythology, Mount Kenya is an Olympus upon which the creator of all things, the god Ngai, has his abode. The religion of Ngai, indeed, is the typical pagan religion of a primitive agricultural people. I would say that, in its normality, its predictability and its perfect suitability to the needs of the Kikuyu, it is not even very original. Ngai is a peasant god to whom requests are made for peace, for a numerous progeny, and for prosperity in the form of healthy livestock and abundant harvests. The character of Ngai is rather that of an authoritarian African paterfamilias, quick to anger and truculent. Ngai has a great deal to do and must not be annoyed with individual requests and prayers; he can occupy himself with his people only in a wholesale manner. The Kikuyu, in fact, say: '*Ngai eikaraga matuine, na nderorangia na wera wa mondo omwe mwanya, eroranagia na mawera ma ando oothe, kana ando a nyomba emwe. Ngai ndegiagiagwo,*' which means: 'God lives in the skies and does not occupy himself with the work and the affairs of one single man. He takes care only of the affairs of a whole people or of a whole clan. The sacrifice and the religion of one single man do not count.' And this, I think, is the most singular aspect of the Kikuyu religion: the rejection of the individual, the prevalent importance of the family, the group, the people.

Otherwise, Ngai behaves like all other pagan gods. He is pleased to accept sacrifices of animals, he imposes a certain number of rites of initiation or celebration, he manifests his power by means of natural phenomena: thunder – to give an example – is the creaking of his bones when he stretches his legs. Apart from Mount Kenya, Ngai has other abodes on other mountains which are therefore sacred. And finally Ngai, like all African divinities, is compromised up to the neck in white and black magic.

Now what point has this simple Kikuyu religion reached? I should say that it was dying. Breached by Islam, which is very active in Kenya, and by Christianity, which however has the disadvantage of being the faith of the whites, it has been destroyed above all by the transformation of the Kikuyu from an agricultural people into a mass of uprooted labourers. This transformation is the result of the policy of expropriation absurdly pursued by the English settlers, that is, precisely by those to whom it should have been of prime importance to preserve the ancestral religion of the Africans as the surest foundation for social peace. In Kenya, during the last years, the same thing has happened, on a small scale, as happened during the early nineteenth century in England, on a large scale, with the Industrial Revolution: the transformation of the peasants into the proletariat, the breakdown of their social order. A farm labourer, a work-man – why should he pray to Ngai? To ask for rain on the land of the white expropriators? Today, from what I am told, the younger generations are abandoning the religion of their ancestors.

But it is dangerous to destroy a religion at a single blow, rather than allow it to die from old age and unreality, especially a primitive religion like that of the Kikuyu, which was at the same time both a faith and a culture. I believe, in fact, that there is no greater suffering for man than to feel his cultural foundations giving way beneath his feet. The destruction of a culture and the pain that spring from it are called, by historians, a 'crisis': the crisis of the ancient world in the age of Hellenism, the crisis of Europe at the time of the Reformation, the crisis of the Western world between the two world wars, and so on. But Europeans, so understanding when it is a question of their own culture, are much less so when faced with cultures different from theirs. For many Englishmen, even if well-intentioned, the drama of the small Kikuyu people is not a crisis but rather the elevation of an African tribe from the obscurity of barbarism to the light of civilization. Owing to these illusions, the social catastrophe of the Kikuyu has been concealed and there has been a direct transition to the tragedy of the Mau Mau.

Nothing can better convey the feeling of incomprehension on the part of the Europeans, when faced with the revolt of the Mau Mau, than the following remark by an English magistrate at the trial of a group of Kikuyu accused of having pronounced the obscene oath of the Mau Mau: 'There is no doubt that the accused, some of whom have had an education, have reverted to the mental and moral state of the Africans at the time of Livingstone.' Now the exact opposite is true: the atrocious violence of the Mau Mau was a new phenomenon due to expropriation and the consequent destruction of the traditional culture. Whereas the Africans, at the time of Livingstone, had, for better or worse, a social and religious order of their own which did not permit this kind of violence.

The truth of this is, in any case, proved even by a super-ficial examination of the Mau Mau revolt. Two aspects of it are immediately striking: first of all the cultural hybridism of the revolt in which, side by side with archaic elements such as ritual cannibalism, others are to be met with, of European type even if distorted and misconceived, such as nationalism, socialism and terrorism. The second feature consists in the self-destructive fury of the Mau Mau: in contrast with less than fifty Europeans killed, tens and tens of thousands of innocent Kikuyu were massacred without pity. How can one fail to recognize in this cultural hybridism and suicidal fury the convulsions of a society in decay which is fighting not so much against foreign masters as against its own internal disintegration?

Why should I have had these thoughts as I walked along the garden paths of the hotel that faces Mount Kenya? Because Mount Kenya, apart from being the mythological abode of the god Ngai, was in recent times the last refuge of Dedan Kimathi, the Mau Mau terrorist who, more than anyone, figured as the incarnation of the mixture of archaic African elements and misconceived European motives which was an essential part of the revolt. I must point out at once, to avoid any misunderstanding, that Dedan Kimathi had nothing whatever to do with political figures of the type of, for instance, Jomo Kenyatta. He was not a political figure who, for his own ends, coldly had recourse to violence and bloodshed, but rather a violent, bloodthirsty man who found in the revolt an opportunity to give vent to his own instincts. But Dedan Kimathi, in a way – the same way, to be quite clear, as the Nazi chiefs – was also an intellectual. Hence the representative character, as I have said, of his personality.

I recall a photograph of Dedan Kimathi, taken at the trial which ended with his death sentence. A cold, pitiless face, with almost Mongol features, with small eyes, high cheekbones, a short, flat nose, a very wide mouth that wore a nauseated expression. It was the face of a proletarian, urban Kikuyu, neither simple nor ingenuous. At school he had been an excellent pupil (the teacher of English had given him a goat as a prize for his skill in poetry) and he had attended the Protestant mission. This gave him the advantage, later, of being able to make use of the Bible as a book of magic well fitted to confer upon him a character of infallibility in the eyes of his followers. He said – and perhaps he himself believed it – that a god had sent it to him from heaven, ready translated into the Kikuyu language, and written especially for him. He had been, furthermore, a soldier, and from his observation of English military discipline had retained some simple and effective notions which were later to come in useful for guerrilla warfare.

But Dedan Kimathi appears also to have been a blood-thirsty, neurotic megalomaniac. He asserted that he was invulnerable, and called himself sometimes, in the English style, 'Sir Dedan Kimathi, Prime Minister', sometimes 'Knight Commandant of the African Empire'. And he, too, like the Mau Mau, turned his fury against his own compatriots rather than against the English. The story of his guerrilla warfare in the forests of Mount Kenya was a story of cruelty of a tyrannical type which at the slightest suspicion, I do not say of betrayal but of mere autonomy, had recourse to death as the sole means of punishment. Thus many of his guerrilla fighters, as well as all the women of his harem except one, perished, strangled personally by him or ordered to be strangled. But Dedan Kimathi was also, as I have mentioned, an intellectual, even if of a deviant kind, who read the Bible to his followers at their reunions in the forest, and commented upon it with colourful oratory. He went around armed with a pencil and paper and gave orders written on the leaves of a notebook; before taking action he consulted a book of magic formulae entitled *Napoleon's Book of Charms*. This partly explains how this bloodthirsty man, of little courage or loyalty, was able to fascinate his disciples right to the end.

After this recollection of Dedan Kimathi, it is perhaps appropriate to describe the hotel built by an American actor, by way of capital investment, right opposite Mount Kenya. Imagine a construction on two floors arranged in a semicircle on a rise in the ground directly facing the sacred mountain. A sort of motel, in fact, from the galleries of which one can enjoy the view of Mount Kenya as one drinks tea or some excellent iced drink. Below the hotel lies a kind of cultivated amphitheatre of green grass, at the bottom of which are the shining dark waters of a small artificial lake. Great white swans swim in this lake, exotic trees with red flowers cast their shadows over it, and cages of African birds are fitted in amongst the branches of the trees. All is clean, bright, reassuring, comfortable, even if somewhat gloomy. But if one goes to the bottom of the garden, in the direction of the mountain, and turns into the asphalt road, very soon one finds oneself confronted by the barrier of a level crossing; and a post carries the notice 'Danger', with a warning not to venture beyond the barrier, into the forest.

The danger to which the notice alludes is, I believe, mainly with regard to the elephants which still live in large numbers in the forest. But one cannot help making a comparison between the situation of the European hotel clinging with its balconies to the formidable flanks of Mount Kenya and that of the thirty thousand settlers who for a short time were under the illusion that they could establish a supremacy of a racist type over a million and a half Kikuyu. In former times, perhaps, this attempt at enslavement might have succeeded. But today it is no longer possible; and it is notable that the ambition of the settlers met with hostility in England even before it did so in Africa. Thus the Mau Mau, with all their bestiality, achieved in a few years what other colonized peoples did not contrive to extort in centuries.

12

The Cross over Africa

Ujiji, January 1969

The car moved slowly forward along a red track – a pale,
damp red like a haemorrhage, as though the rubble had
become mingled with blood. We were crossing the belt of
cultivated land that lies between the high plateau and Lake
Tanganyika. Vegetable gardens, fields, flower gardens;
everything was of a spongy, brilliant green; and here and
there, mango-trees like dark balloons moored in mid-air.
This was the first sign of cultivation we had seen after
driving for two days through the bush of the plateau.
This part of Tanzania, on the borders of Burundi, is wild
without being really picturesque or really exotic. At some
points the bush was reminiscent of the *maquis* of the
Apennines. Only the dazzling, crude light, blinding after
downpours of rain, reminded us that we were in Africa.

We came in sight of Lake Tanganyika. It appeared
suddenly between two hills, which widened out and drew
apart until the lake spread and invaded the horizon. It was
black beneath a roof of the black clouds of the rainy season.
The boundaries of its deserted water could not be seen (Lake
Tanganyika is about as wide and as long as the Adriatic),
but one feels that it is nevertheless a lake because from it
there is not the faintest breath of the free, moving, uncon-
fined air that characterizes the sea. In fact, to tell the
truth, it arouses a feeling, almost, of claustrophobia. Lake
Tanganyika is in truth the navel of Africa, a navel fifteen
hundred metres deep set in the belly of the continent, many
days' journey, by untrodden tracks, both from the Indian
Ocean and the Atlantic. Nor would the painful feeling of a

cul-de-sac be in any way lessened by crossing the lake and reaching the opposite shore. Over there is the Congo: more uninhabited bush country, more blood-coloured tracks.

According to a local legend, Lake Tanganyika was originally a small, deep well, the property of a couple, man and wife. The gods had filled the well with choice fish; but this was a secret which was not to be known. The wife took a lover, told him about the fish and gave him some of them to eat. The gods, irritated, caused the well to overflow; husband, wife, and lover were drowned, the well continued to overflow and became Tanganyika, the third largest lake in the world. Some may see in this legend the structural element of secrecy and of feminine indiscretion. I myself see in it, above all, the poverty of the Africans. Who can tell? The married couple was perhaps the first Bantu tribe to put in an appearance on the shores of the lake, which teems with fish (according to ichthyologists it contains one hundred and forty-six varieties). Conscious of its good fortune, the tribe must have wished to guard the secret of this fishy wealth. But another tribe must have arrived on the scene and so finally the secret was divulged.

We reached Ujiji. It was here, according to history (our European history) that, on 10 November 1871, Doctor Livingstone, ill and carried on a stretcher by his faithful Negro servants, met Stanley, the correspondent sent by Bennett, editor of the *New York Herald*, in search of the missionary. It was at Ujiji that the dialogue between the two explorers, as celebrated as it is ridiculous (with a ridiculousness characteristic of Victorian sublimity) took place: 'Doctor Livingstone, I presume?'

'Yes.'

'I thank God, Doctor, who has allowed me to see you.'

'And I am grateful to you for being here and I bid you welcome.'

According to a big book I read as a boy, *In Search of the Sources of the Nile*, adorned with numerous copperplate engravings, the meeting and the conversation took place in the depths of a forest little less than virgin. In reality the place is very different. We left the track and turned into a rough secondary road, between two rows of rectangular huts of chocolate-coloured dried mud with rusty sheet-iron roofs. The car went bumping down the steep, rough road which looked like the bed of a torrent, towards the tiny harbour on the lake where the wharf could be seen, down below, with a few boats secured among the reeds. But we did not go to the harbour; we stopped all of a sudden on a small level space. Here – a strange thing in that dreary, nameless spot – stands a small monument, a kind of truncated pyramid of mustard-coloured blocks of stone. On one face of the pyramid, carved in relief, can be seen the blunt, massive African continent which so closely resembles its bluntest, most massive animal, the rhinoceros. On top of the continent, almost wiping it out, is superimposed, in relief, a big black Christian cross, the extremities of which reach Tripoli at the top and Cape Town at the bottom.

I bent down to read the memorial tablet: 'Here stood the mango-tree under which, on November 10th 1871, Henry Morton Stanley met Doctor David Livingstone.'

I looked round. It must be admitted that the Africans do not appear to attribute the same importance to the meeting as the Europeans. The whole place is strewn with pieces of excrement swarming with black, blue and green flies. The weedy grass is filthy and trampled. A troop of almost naked children, with astonished faces, gazed at us with apprehension and amazement: it would seem that not many Europeans turn up at Ujiji. We got back into the car and went down to the harbour. There was a large boat, worn out and full of fetid water, drawn up among the tall grass; there were a few canoes, hollowed-out trunks of trees; there were some fishermen who, at the sight of our cameras, made ugly faces and threatening gestures at us. We photographed the lake which, for a moment, with its green beds of delicate reeds and a flight of a few flamingoes, suggested an ancient Chinese print; then we left. Good-bye to Ujiji.

But the Christian cross superimposed so securely over the entire African continent gives food for thought. Its symbolic character is exceedingly inexact: the Christian religion, perhaps because it is the religion of the European invaders, has by no means conquered Africa. It would appear that the greatest progress has been made by Islam which, anyhow, is the religion of the Arabs, the traditional butchers of the African peoples. But Islam is a simpler religion than Christianity. In it the relationship with God is more direct, and without intermediaries. Finally Islam is 'immovable'; Christianity, on the other hand 'moves', it has not stopped 'moving' ever since its beginnings. So that today the former, having remained a religion in the traditional sense, attracts the Africans more than the latter, which is often reduced to moral philosophy. But this is not the point round which my thoughts revolve.

To put it briefly, the great question is: was it necessary to 'discover' Africa? And in any case what is the real meaning of the verb 'to discover'? Let us consider the matter. There is the scholar who, after long and passionate research, 'discovers', in the course of it, an ancient text; and then there is the neo-*avant-garde* enthusiast who, thanks to a tardy translation, 'discovers' Joyce's *Ulysses* thirty years after its original publication. The first is humble: he studies the book he is reading, identifies himself with it, obliterates himself in it; the second is presumptuous: in 'discovering' Joyce he imagines he is creating him, inventing him, and thus, instead of discovering him, he effaces him, he conceals him. Now the 'discovery' of Africa belongs to this second category. What, in reality, did the nineteenth-century explorers discover? Nothing truly African (except, perhaps, the actual configuration of places). To such a degree that it might be positively asserted that the explorers, instead of 'discovering' Africa, 'covered it up'. They covered it up with European 'civilization', to allow time to those who came after them – the generals and adventurers, the profiteers and the businessmen – to invade the unfortunate continent, to occupy it, to subdue it, to divide it into lots, without scruple and without sense of guilt.

Today it is at last being realized that the 'discovery' of Africa was in reality the ingenuous, irresistible biological thrust of stronger peoples to the detriment of weaker peoples. But the trauma has occurred, irreparably. It is hard to see why, when the barbarian invasions of the late Middle Ages and the Islamic oppression of India are deplored, the European expansion in Africa during the nineteenth century should be considered a fundamentally advantageous fact. In reality this expansion has been a painful fracture, a brutal introduction of a foreign body, a grievous intrusion, possibly a decisive, final deviation.

Africa ought to have been allowed time. Tribal culture, at the same time extremely widespread and extremely fragmentary, should have been allowed to organize itself in a continental sense, not artificially constricted within the arbitrary limits of imaginary nations which had never existed, on the European model, with all the vexations characteristic of that model: bureaucratic centralization, nationalism, armies, frontiers, custom-houses, police forces and so on. As Julius Nyerere, President of Tanzania, once said: 'Tanganyika is a completely artificial country. We have a hundred and ten tribes. We might have less or we might have more. I have never understood why at a certain point men cease to be Tanzanians and become Kenyans, Congolese, Ugandans.' Let me add, however, that by now it is not even certain that the pan-African solution is the right one. All is confused, muddled, obscured, clouded by a thousand enormous difficulties of all kinds. The only thing that is really certain is that the whole of Africa is in an eruptive, explosive, effervescent condition.

13

Rags and Uniforms

Kigoma, February 1969

It was evening, and already twilight, at Kigoma. I went and sat on the terrace of the hotel, centre of the town's social life, in one of the three or four groups of rusty tubular chairs and tables of which its equipment is composed. The terrace juts out to some extent over the street, so that I could have a comprehensive view of Kigoma, the largest urban centre of the immense, deserted region of the same name which extends along Lake Tanganyika. For indeed Kigoma is all here in this sort of 'main street' – two rows of houses of only one floor, lined up along the two sides of the street, in the sultry shade of gigantic mango-trees with dark, gloomy foliage. Banks, offices, shops, public buildings are all to be found in these detached houses with little rickety porches and walls painted grass green, aniline blue or canary yellow, the only colours of paint to be found in this part of Africa, or so it would seem, judging by their widespread use. The Kigoma main street starts from the station square and comes to an end at the market square, five hundred metres farther up. Kigoma is a town beset by solitude and lack of communications. The train that makes a three-day journey to Dar-es-Salaam runs only three times a week; once a week there is a steamer which leaves Kigoma for Albertville, on the opposite shore of the lake, fifty kilometres away. There are, of course, the tracks; but they enforce hourly averages of twenty or thirty kilometres and one can travel for as much as two days without finding hotels. As for aeroplanes, there is an airport at Ujiji near by, but no airline makes it a starting-point. All this explains

73

the 'dated' appearance of Kigoma, as a small town of the period of early colonialism whose pioneer, here, was the Germany of Kaiser Wilhelm.

Nairobi, capital of Kenya, and Kampala, capital of Uganda, are small, very modern, clean, bright towns which would not make a bad impression in California; the somewhat surprising creations of neo-capitalism, that is to say, of neo-colonialism. At Kigoma, on the other hand, there is still the atmosphere of the so-called 'mysterious' Africa, in other words the definitely backward and poverty-stricken Africa, the Africa of Livingstone who wished to convert the Africans to Christianity and of Bismarck's generals who exterminated them because they rejected the benefits of Germanic *Kultur*. Kigoma is the 'Far West' of Tanzania; its character of a 'frontier town' is clearly revealed by its shops which are all the property of Indians. No polished shop-windows, no rationalized display of goods, no so to speak 'specialized' shops in which only one species of article is sold, as in Nairobi or Kampala; but dark storehouses in which, as in the old-fashioned drugstores of the American West, there is a bit of everything, from medicines to textiles, from ironmongery to hats, from perfumes to ready-made clothes. It does not need much imagination to see that these dark warehouses squeeze out all the money there is in the region. Apart from anything else, this is shown by the numerous quite luxurious bungalows which the Indian proprietors of these shops have built for themselves on the hills behind Kigoma, in sight of the lake.

At the moment, since it was late afternoon, the shops were closed; and the merchants were walking up and down the main street of Kigoma. It was promenading time, as in Italy and, in general, in countries with a mild climate. It was an interesting spectacle, if only because it revealed the social composition of the town. The promenaders were all Indians, which is as much as to say that the whole of the town's middle class was Indian. Plump, bearded men, dressed in white, wearing turbans; slender young men in long, dark tunics with closed collars. Walking with dignity beside them, looking like big, sharp-eyed caterpillars, the women, wrapped in the vaporous gauze of their saris, lilac or amethyst, aquamarine blue, pearl grey. These middle-class shopkeepers walk gravely, slowly, with a satisfied air, enjoying, if not exactly the evening air (the heat is suffocating), at least a well-deserved relaxation after the stress of the day's business. But they are all Indians; of Africans, not a sign.

To see the Africans, one must get up early in the morning and watch the procession of proletarians going to work at the harbour, at the station, at the building yards, at the little sugar and sisal factories. In the evening the Indians walk gravely and slowly and dressed in their best clothes; in the morning, the Africans hurry along barefoot, dressed in rags, with the worried, absorbed faces of people who have to keep to a time-table and are afraid of being late. The manner of dressing of this African proletariat is worthy of an exhaustive study, especially the pullovers and sleeveless vests that the men wear above their tattered trousers. Some of these pullovers are merely symbolical, so many are the holes in them and so exiguous the sound material. One can imagine a workman getting up in his bare hut (the huts contain nothing but a mat for sleeping on and a few baskets in which are kept the most necessary objects, all higgledy-piggledy) and putting on his fine vest. This garment has a hole in the back as big as the back of the man and, in front, innumerable holes which uncover more than they cover. How does the man manage to find the right hole? And why does he wear a vest like this? What purpose does it serve?

Indians and Africans. They have no social contact, they do not eat together, they do not intermarry. The Indians are racists, not of the present day but from thousands of years back; not individually and by chance, but on the basis of a centuries-old social system; for that reason it is not difficult to imagine what they think of the Africans. As for the latter, their attitude is complex. Nothing could be more characteristic of this complexity than the verdict on the rich Indians given by an extremely poor, ragged African: 'They are not intelligent.' From which there emerges, not so much a political or class resentment, as a difference in the conception of life, in vision of the world.

Colonialism in Tanzania was quietly reproducing the caste structures of India. Caste in India is called *varna*; and *varna* also means colour, that is, colour of skin. As in India, the identification of social function with colour of skin was also taking place in Tanzania, even though in a more simplified manner. At the top, and in power, were the Europeans, first the Germans, later the English, white and fair-haired with blue eyes; below them, as traders and intermediaries, came the Indians, the Arabs, the Levantines, not quite so white but not black either; finally, on the lowest step of the social scale, the proletarians, all of them black, completely black. African nationalism has put an end to this species of *apartheid* which, though liberal, was no less discriminatory than the South African type.

But nationalism could never have got rid of caste racism without socialism. Here one encounters the difference between European and African socialism. In Europe socialism has always been internationalist; in Africa, on the other hand, it provides an indispensable constituent element for nationalism which, without it, could not but become an instrument of neo-colonialism. In some cases, this has happened.

In Tanzania, Africanization of society has been dealt with by the 'Arusha Charter'. In this fine town in the Kilimanjaro area, President Julius Nyerere has sought, by means of this Charter, to provide an ideological justification for a number of provisions for nationalization of the banks, of the import–export trade, of insurance and so on. The Indians, who monopolize trade, will have to leave by degrees, from today until 1972 and beyond, as in Kenya.

The 'Arusha Charter' (as, in Manzoni's *The Betrothed*, the lawyer Azzeccagarbugli says with regard to the edicts against the 'bravoes and vagabonds') speaks clearly: 'In order to build socialism, it is necessary that the workmen and the peasants should be in power and should control the means of .production.' Now we shall have to see whether this Charter which, among other things, provides for the nationalization of the land and the rearrangement of the rural economy on co-operative bases, as well as the end 'of the exploitation of the country districts by the towns' – we shall have to see, I say, whether these reforms will be effected from below, with the gradualness and thoroughness of a real grip of social and political conscience, or from above, by the usual authoritarian methods of governments which rely for their support on a single party. In Tanzania, as is well known, there is in fact a single party, the TANU, that is, the Tanganyika African National Union.

Julius Nyerere, the cultivated, up-to-date President of Tanzania, seems to wish to proceed in a democratic manner. Tanzania, in the last four years, has been seen to promulgate no less than four constitutions. Naturally, if there is to be democracy, it will be a question of a socialist-type democracy, to some extent 'Chinese', that is, brought up to date on the model of the 'cultural revolution', though in a less rigid, less ideological way than in China. The Chinese Red Guards here become Green Guards; socialism is termed *Ujamaa*, that is, brotherhood; and Julius Nyerere, the the charismatic head of state in Tanzania, is designated by the affectionate nickname of *Mwlamu* or 'schoolteacher'. We are not so very far from Mao, or at least from the paternal, didactic Mao put forward by the cultural revolution in China.

The danger, as already mentioned, is the repressive, military authoritarianism to which, for historical and ethnical reasons, all the young African nations are exposed. In Tanzania, for example, there is certainly one of the best dressed, most efficient and most respected police forces in all Africa. Even in the most remote villages, amongst the half-naked crowd, the flies and the dust of the markets, I have seen policemen dressed like English colonels, with immaculate, pressed, even starched uniforms. They represent something more than order: they represent the State – and they know it. I recall a visit to the police station of a remote small country town, for an inspection of passports. The rooms were clean and airy, the shelves full of notebooks piled up in perfect order. There were even a couple of

77

women in uniform, with light-coloured jackets and black skirts; there were several policemen, who all spoke English and who appeared to have laid down long-standing rules for the correct 'tone': a mixture of bureaucratic courtesy and military rigidity. In the first room, one whole corner was occupied by a great iron cage. Inside the cage, standing up with his hands tied to the bars, there was a single prisoner who had just been arrested, a petty thief, probably. He was a boy of under twenty, and he looked at us with enormous black and white eyes and an expression of anguish. He was heart-broken, one felt, at not understanding why he was there. He represented the Africa that is innocent even if criminal, stupefied even if malicious, the Africa that finds itself suddenly plunged into modern civilization, faced with the new fetishes of repression, of education, of efficiency and of nationalism.

14

The End of Prehistory

After a series of bends on a steeply rising road through a forest with a strange mixture of Alpine conifers and tropical trees, we came to a stop on a level space and got out. The air was cool and pure; before us a wide view opened out, luminous, remote, unreal. It was an immense valley of a pale, almost colourless, misty green. A valley completely deserted, covered with fine grass, with the blue eye of a lake at the bottom. But it was not like other valleys. Generally the African plains seem boundless, they seem to go beyond the horizon. Here, on the other hand, the eye, after skimming over the expanse of grass, suddenly encounters a wall, a wall that is also green and unreal. The eye travels up along this wall, reaches its edge, follows it and then realizes that the valley is not a valley but the crater of an extinct volcano. This is Ngorongoro, one of the biggest volcanic craters in the world. And at the same time it is a game reserve, or, as they call it here, a sanctuary of African fauna.

A little later we went bumping down over the stones and pot-holes of a path leading towards the bottom of the crater. The farther down we went, the wider and deeper the crater became. The grassy walls rose up and retreated, the flat plain spread out on all sides. It is so vast that one sees, even at a glance, how the most diverse species of animals can live there side by side, ignorant of each others' presence. First, a herd of zebra. Showily striped in black and white, their camouflage seems useless in so exposed a place; they look as if they were painted. Slowly they move across the track; they are large, rotund, massive, capacious, striped barrels with four legs and a head. Nature's brush-work has been careful: on their hindquarters the stripes do not coincide with those on their tails. A little farther on, a troop of gazelles explodes, as it were, leaping sideways, frightened by the car; these pretty little animals bound upwards as though propelled into the air by invisible springs. Then we left the track and plunged into marshy ground, dark beneath tall green trees. Then, bright, luminous, whitish grassland, flooded with light. A small, dark spot, far away but obviously heavy and curious in shape was pointed out to us by our guide: it was a rhino-ceros, or rather *the* rhinoceros – not more than one is ever seen and its rarity leads always to the conclusion that it is the sole survivor of the species. It was grazing peacefully: while its mouth sought grass on the ground, its horn, meanwhile, threatened the sky.

We continued on our way. Half of the crater was now in sunshine and the other half in the shadow of a sudden storm-cloud. Where there was sunshine, there was dazzling light; where there was shadow, the greenness of the crater was already dimmed by the livid streaks of rain from a cloud-burst. But the animals take no notice of the rain; like the rain, they are a part of nature. Down below – a sight just as thrilling as the sight of the rhinoceros – were three or four black specks barely visible above the tall, pale grass. These were buffaloes, said to be the most dangerous animals in Africa. I would have liked to go nearer, to take a long look at their black horns, flat and curving down-wards so that they frame their heads and form a kind of ebony vizor over their eyes. But it was not possible. Buffaloes are angry beasts and they charge, head down, with unforeseen suddenness.

My companions, of course, wanted to see some lions. Personally, I am not enthusiastic about lions. There are too many of them in heraldry and in the circuses of Europe. The lion, as a result of being emblematic, has become almost domestic. It is true that it is the beast which best incarnates and expresses what has usually come to be called nobility, both in the bearing and the formation of its head and body. I myself prefer the fantastic, unbelievable giraffe. The lion is not typical of Black Africa, as is the giraffe. After all, only a few centuries ago lions inhabited Libya and Algeria, that is, the shores of the Mediterranean. But the giraffe is as improbable as the mythical unicorn. Still today, if you see the long necks of giraffes, far away in the glaring light of a pallid waste, rising here and there like exclamation marks between heaven and earth (their heads are always turned in the opposite direction to that of their bodies) – if you see a row of giraffes motionless on the line of the horizon, then you will know for certain that you are in Africa.

Wandering in zigzag fashion over the grassland, we went looking for lions. Then, all of a sudden, a lion appeared. Or rather, it was a lioness. She was lying on her back, her legs in the air, almost across our track. Her head lay lolling in the grass, her eyes closed; her soft, white paunch seemed troubled by a repeated gasping, and a large bloodstained hole was visible close to her groin. The lioness had been wounded, by a rhinoceros or a buffalo perhaps; and by instinct she was seeking to heal the wound by exposing the hole made by the horn-thrust to the sun. We watched her for some time, pitying her and thinking that she was in her death agony. But all of a sudden she raised her head, yawned in a manner that was not in the least painful and then rose to her feet. She paused, then walked slowly away through the grass, then went and lay down again a few yards further away.

At a short distance from the wounded lioness and no doubt from other lions, her nearest relatives, which we did not see, a small herd of gnu was grazing – those curious bearded, horned animals with low hindquarters and tall heads. Once again I was struck by the peaceful proximity of the lions and their habitual prey. The gnu, as well as the zebras, antelopes and gazelles, are conscious of the fact that there are lions only a few steps away; as also, the naked, unarmed Masai herdsmen whom we could see, not so very far off, wandering slowly round their cattle; and yet not the slightest fear seemed to affect either animals or men. It may be that fear is not the exception, but the rule, in Africa. And since it is the rule, it has become transformed into a calm, even though cautious, knowledge of danger. The gnu, the zebras, the antelopes, the gazelles know, not consciously but instinctively, when, how and why the lions attack. They know it so well, so infallibly, that they can afford to graze under the noses of their enemies. This, I believe, partly explains the strange peace of Africa, the feeling of majestic, tragic serenity that emanates from the African landscape.

But it is also true that this landscape has a very special character that is not to be found in any other part of the world. Geologists maintain that the African continent is the most ancient of all; that is to say, that it was the first to emerge from the primordial ocean and the first to be subjected to unwitting moulding by erosion. This may be so, in fact it is so. But these boundless, deserted plains, bordered by very low, table-shaped hills, this dazzling light, these profound silences, all these – not, it may be thought, by chance – together with the presence of wild animals, go to compose a complete picture of the world of prehistory. It is possible that what the deplorable rhetoric of base exoticism has for a long time called the 'Africa sickness' was really the nostalgia, well known to all those who have travelled in Africa, for a world in which not merely is there no visible sign of history but in which prehistory still holds undisputed sway. History in Europe and Asia certainly does not seem to weigh heavily; it is, so to speak, in the air. But as soon as you find yourself in Africa, the relief which you cannot help feeling proves that both Western and Eastern man are intoxicated with history. Prehistory, in spite of its terrors, may then appear as a refuge.

Only for a short time, however. On our return from the crater of Ngorongoro we were all extremely pleased at having seen, gathered together in so small a space, so much African fauna; instead, we ought to have felt sad. These so-called 'sanctuaries' of African fauna, the minute green patches of which are mere spots on maps of the continent, these 'reserves' in which thousands of animals live in undisturbed freedom (but watched over by bodies of State foresters), are in reality an indication of the approaching death of prehistory in Africa, of the impending triumph of history. In ten, twenty, or, at most, thirty years the Africa of prehistory will no longer exist. It is a simple question of financial and demographic expansion. Black Africa is a plateau of one to two thousand metres in height, habitable everywhere, often ideally healthy and fertile. North America has taken a century and a half to transform its deserts into a populous nation. The analogous metamorphosis of Africa will certainly be more rapid. It is not science fiction but reasonable foresight to imagine the African bush being levelled tomorrow by bulldozers and changed, with chemical fertilizers, into good cultivated land; the villages, with their huts full of flies and dust and infections, replaced by groups of buildings made of concrete and glass and steel; the tracks covered with asphalt; a multiplication of air traffic; and the dark plateau, in short, transmuted into something fine and commonplace and modern like California. A similar transformation has already been started in Uganda and Kenya. Meanwhile, while we wait for the metamorphosis to be completed, the game reserves notify us not so much of the precarious safety of the fauna of the present day as of the extermination of the fauna of the past. The whole of Tanzania, for instance, before its colonization by the Germans, was a single reserve. When the Germans built the railway from Dar-es-Salaam to Kigoma, the lions, then very numerous throughout Tanganyika, were exterminated, partly in order to protect the workmen, partly out of hunters' sadism – exterminated, according to the words of an English traveller of the period, 'like vermin'. And the same thing happened in the case of the elephants, the rhinoceros, the buffaloes, the leopards. The young African States know that, as well as their sunshine, they can sell, at a high price, their fauna. So there will be a multiplication of safaris, which allow any rich man from Via Montenapoleone or Fifth Avenue to murder an elephant or a lion (for murder it is, given the beauty, the grandeur and the innocence of the animal and the complete lack of risk to the hunter). Until the total extinction of the species is reached. Africa, in short, is on the point of vanishing for ever. This is already shown by the change in African terminology. A century ago Africa was 'mysterious'. Today it is merely 'depressed'.

15

Spies and Photographers

Tabora, February 1969

We left Mwanza, on Lake Victoria, very late: our departure
had been fixed for nine o'clock and we started at eleven.
Then we took the wrong road just outside Mwanza, going
in the direction of Musoma instead of towards Biharamulo.
At the Busisi ferry (Lake Victoria, as big as Ireland, at this
point becomes a marshy inlet as wide as the Po) we wasted
two hours under a scorching sun, looking at an old, half-
sunken ferry-boat while the good one was still on the
opposite bank. Later, we waited for Pier Paolo Pasolini (the
film he was to make for Italian Television had been the
pretext for my journey in Tanzania) to take photographs, at
his leisure, of the African landscape (the circular villages of
the Masai, baobabs of monstrous size, fantastic piles of
rocks like colossal mango fruits heaped up on top of one
another by the hand of a giant). Finally the punctures. We
were travelling in two cars, a Land-Rover which never
punctures but goes slowly and a town saloon which goes
fast but punctures. Four punctures in one afternoon. All
this, not counting the delay for lunch, a stop to purchase
the spear of a Masai herdsman, a halt at another minor
ferry. We should have arrived at Kibondo before nightfall;
we reached it in darkness. On the road map Kibondo bears
a reassuring sign: a little house with a cross inside it. This
means: Furnished Rest-house. If the house had no cross
inside it, it would mean: Rest-house without furniture.

Here, then, was Kibondo. It was nine o'clock, but the
inhabitants of Kibondo, like all the peasants in the world,
were already in bed; the little town seemed lifeless and

asleep. We went round among the huts, along the avenues of mango-trees, and came out into a crooked, asymmetrical open space surrounded by tumbledown hovels and lit by a single lamp-post. In the middle was a petrol-pump and a lorry with its headlights turned off. But a streak of light shone from under the lowered shutter of an Indian shop. We knocked and shouted: and finally the shopkeeper and his family came and opened the shutter. All four of them were in their pyjamas; the shop was in darkness but the room behind the shop was lit up and the whole family were sitting at a big table eating their national curry.

The Indians turned on the lights in the shop, while one of them went to work the petrol-pump and the others attended to our purchases. Buying is a way of communicating; and after a day's drive through the uninhabited bush we were anxious to communicate and in fact bought all sorts of things: cotton materials with barbaric colours and designs but made in Manchester; tinned foodstuffs both local and foreign; bottles of Danish beer; Scotch whisky in travelling flasks; aspirin and anti-mosquito ointment; thin, black Tanzanian cigarettes; even an object for playing jokes on other people, an indiarubber snake that moved of itself and looked as if it were alive. We filled up with petrol, paid for our purchases and left.

Again we drove round Kibondo for some little time, until finally we met a man walking in the dark and carrying a big river-fish on a hook. With complete assurance, he pointed out a road to us. We drove along it and found ourselves in front of a closed gate surmounted by a cross. A church, perhaps, or a mission, or even a cemetery? There was no knowing. We turned back and came upon a company of night-wanderers. They stopped, questioned us, commented on our replies, discussed things among themselves, hesitated, asked who we were and where we were going and where we had come from and what we were doing, then discussed the matter between themselves again. It was clear that they were in no hurry and that our presence was – what shall I call it? – a social occasion in the absolute isolation of

Kibondo, which must be exploited to the greatest possible extent.

Finally the information we were requiring was provided with an abundance of detail: we left hurriedly and found ourselves in front of a house. We waited a long time, a quarter of an hour perhaps. At last a very well-dressed young man appeared, wearing a new pullover and well-pressed trousers: for him, too, our presence was a social event; he had kept us waiting in order to perform his toilet and put on his best clothes. Courteous and self-assured, he got into our car, directed us out of Kibondo and up a hill, and then into a garden.

By the light of our headlamps we could see a tumble-down hut, with windows barred and a door smothered in creepers. An old caretaker emerged from somewhere or other, and with difficulty opened the door which appeared not to have been unlocked for years. There was no electricity, but by the light of a pocket lamp we caught sight of the dusty floors and dark walls of three little rooms that smelt mouldy and stuffy. The furnishings promised by the road map consisted of two sets of bed-springs, one of which was provided with a thin little mattress, three chairs, a broken-down armchair and a table. There was no kitchen; the bathroom consisted of a shower set in grey cement of a military type. We sat down at the table and, with a complete lack of knives, forks, spoons, plates or glasses, ate almost in darkness, taking greasy pieces of corned beef in our fingers and gulping down draughts of warm orangeade straight from the bottle. Then we went to bed, some on the bed-springs, some on the floor, and some on the seats of the saloon car in the garden.

Next morning, scattered here and there about the rooms, we woke up with aching bones. Magnificent, indiscreet sunshine crudely showed up the dust on the floors, the cracked plaster, the disembowelled tins and empty bottles all over the table. We hurriedly left Kibondo without pausing for breakfast, except for a few sips of orangeade or whisky. Again we drove along a red, blood-coloured track like an unclosed wound, through bush country of frantic sunlight and tangled shrubs like small trees. We drove slowly, to avoid punctures; then stopped at a small market that seemed like a public dance-hall. Inside a high stockade, close-packed and jostling, was a half-naked crowd, compact and almost motionless, head to head, chest to chest, belly to belly, leg to leg, taking part in the market more from a need for social contact, it seemed, than in order to buy anything, as though the market were a kind of cocktail party. Pasolini, of course, pointed his camera at them; and, equally naturally, a police jeep arrived from somewhere or other. The inspector, a tall, very thin, lanky man, with a small, bearded, curly head, took the two drivers aside and gave them a good scolding in Swahili. Then he went away without deigning to look at us. The explanation was that it was not permitted to photograph anything that might give a prejudicial idea of life in Tanzania. We got back into the car and left.

We came to a notice-board marked 'Kasulu'. This little town showed itself at once to be a place of extreme poverty. There was a large market-place with some streets running out of it. But the market was a dusty, sun-scorched space in which some half-naked old women, squatting here and there on the ground, were selling a few bananas or blackish, fly-covered pieces of meat. Round the square, the usual huts contained the usual Indian shops; the streets, beyond a few hovels, died away in the bush. Kasulu appeared deserted; but as soon as our two cars came to a stop, we were immediately surrounded by a crowd, mostly of women and boys. I looked at the aged sellers in the market and reflected that complete nudity in Africa was rather like the tiny feet in China: nowadays it was only the old women belonging to the early colonial generation who showed their bosoms; the young ones cover them up. Meanwhile Pasolini, taking no notice of the recent warning as to the inadvisability of taking photographs of the less modern aspects of the country, had hoisted his cine-camera and was filming everything: the squalid, dusty market; the squatting old women with their long, flat breasts like empty pockets; the bony, mangy dogs lying in the sun; the wretched merchandise, the ragged beggars and the naked children. The crowd surrounded him, a smiling, friendly, ingenuous, good-natured crowd. Then, all of a sudden, a freezing blast caused all this cordiality and cheerfulness to vanish. A man in a white shirt, a man who was absolutely black but with almost Caucasian features, and with a bristling military moustache and angry eyes, accosted us in a voice of thunder, shouting, in Swahili, things that were incomprehensible but obviously unpleasant. In his bearing, his harshness and his air of authority he appeared to be an ex-military man, a soldier trained in the discipline of the British army; that moustache, identical but red – I have seen it on the upper lip of more than one British colonel. He was supported by a young man who looked like a student or an intellectual, undersized, plump, unctuous, smiling, treacherous and full of hatred, who repeated in good English what the man with the moustache was shouting in Swahili. What was it all about, in any case? The fact was that they were accusing us of being spies; of having made the journey all the way from Rome to Kasulu to carry out espionage to the detriment of Tanzania.

The crowd was no longer smiling now; it could be felt perfectly well that its mood was changing from irrational sympathy to an equally irrational antipathy. The man with the moustache thundered, the intellectual sought to intimidate us with his English; someone had a good idea and proposed that we should go, the whole lot of us, to the police station, away from the crowd which had now become threatening. No sooner said than done; we took our accusers into the car and left the square. At the police station, a young officer, twisting and turning our passports in his hands, listened with an air of embarrassment to the invectives of the man with the moustache and the insinuations of the intellectual. Our two enemies did all they could to have us arrested and locked up, for a few hours at least, in the big iron cage that occupied one corner of the room; but the arrival of the inspector altered the situation in our favour. Smiling, bureaucratic, competent, this middle-aged man with a good-natured face cast a glance at the passports and

and then let us go. We distributed cigarettes and hand-shakes to everyone, including our two adversaries, and then left again.

As our two cars moved away along the track, inevitable reflections occurred to me. The accusation of espionage was, fundamentally, a sign of the backwardness of this part of Tanzania. Spy-mania is one of the many gifts of national-ism, it raged in Europe during the war of 1914: but Fascism, twenty years later, tried in vain to resuscitate it with its posters showing a grim English soldier holding his hand to an enormous scarlet ear. Thus it was that the man with the moustache and the intellectual were fifty years behind the times – a reasonable lapse of time, after all, considering the utter isolation of this part of Africa.

16

An African Puppet-show

Dodoma, March 1969

It was raining; and I went to sit in the bar. We were on the
point of leaving Kigoma, our suitcases were ready, the
three-times-a-week train for Dodoma would be starting in
little more than an hour. I settled myself on top of a stool
and looked out through the dirty windows into the courtyard, where the waiters were busying themselves, absurdly,
in putting out clothes to dry in the rain. The bar was
almost in darkness, and it was extremely hot; I ordered a
beer from the barman-cum-manager of the hotel, an Indian
with a conical head in the shape of a projectile, a projectile
with eyes of a clear, sweet, indeed honey-sweet, blackness,
downcast with a perpetually melting and melancholy
expression. He was fat, this manager, with a fat stomach
rather than a paunch, as happens with those who drink a
great deal. He drank, in fact, all day long, as he himself
admitted, as he in turn poured out a beer for himself, the
tenth, he said, of the morning. He drank and repeated:
'So you're leaving our beautiful Kigoma,' brooding over
me with his molasses eyes as though he really felt distressed
at our departure.

An African, whom I had met the previous evening, came
and sat beside me. He was the director of the local agency of
the Congolese shipping line, whose ships go twice a week to
Albertville, on the opposite shore of Lake Tanganyika. The
following dialogue took place between us:

'Yesterday evening you called me your very dear brother
and assured me that you would arrange for me to have a
visa for the Congo so that I would be able to leave for

91

Albertville today. You also made an appointment with me for nine o'clock this morning. I went to the office at the time arranged and you were not to be found. What is to be done about it?'

'Albertville, a magnificent town! It's a pity, it's really a pity that you're not going to Albertville. And the lake crossing, too, is extremely interesting.'

'I'm sure it is. But you were not to be found. And a German employee of yours told me that it's absolutely impossible to obtain a visa for a week, at least.'

'He's not German, he's Dutch. Albertville: a very big town, very, very beautiful. You ought to visit it.'

'Forgive my insisting, but was your promise to get me a visa for the Congo by any chance a generous illusion caused by whisky and beer?'

'Albertville – a marvellous town!'

'Yesterday evening you were drunk. This morning you woke up in your right mind, you remembered your promise and you disappeared. Isn't that so?'

'Albertville, a much finer town than Kigoma.'

As on the previous evening, he kept his hand pressed affectionately on mine. The manager gazed at the two of us without saying a word, with those melancholy, honey-sweet eyes. I was no longer capable of enduring so much sweetness. I rose abruptly and went to take a walk in the rain.

I went round behind the hotel and started up the road with its panoramic view and, on either side, the luxurious villas of the Indian traders. It was raining slightly with a gentle rustling sound on the gloomy foliage of the mango-trees. And then, at a bend in the road, I saw the lake. It was the colour of lead, grey and opaque, but of lead in which numbers of thin, sparkling streaks had been cut with the point of a knife. A mass of black clouds hung above the horizon which itself, however, was clear and luminous. Two Africans approached and walked along on either side of me. One of them, the younger one, had a round, good-natured face; the other was older, with a thin face made longer by a goatee beard, and a saturnine, peevish expression. This latter man started a conversation in English. He pointed to the watch on my wrist and asked me if I wished to sell it: 'Shall we do some business, then? I value it very highly. I'll give you twenty shillings.'

'Thank you, I'm not selling it. It's very useful to me.'

'You can go back to England and buy a better one with my twenty shillings.'

'I'm not selling it; it was a present, a family souvenir.'

'Twenty is too much, certainly. But I like you. I want you to be pleased.'

'There's no question of it.'

'It's worth, roughly, five shillings. I will give you twenty. No one in your place would hesitate.'

Full of resentment, he smiled; he said something in Swahili to his companion; then, without ceremony, he seized my wrist and tried to slip off the watch. I pulled my wrist away vigorously. He took no notice but seized my wrist again and said to his young companion: 'What d'you think about this watch? Don't you think twenty shillings is too much?'

The young one sniggered. This time, as well as pulling away my wrist, I gave this aggressive would-be buyer a good push. In his hand he had a small knife with which, when we met, he had been cutting the bough of a tree to make a stick. He almost lost his balance, looked at me sideways, made some exclamation, rather threateningly, in Swahili. At that moment a little Indian girl, sheltering under an immense green umbrella, came towards us along the road. The African turned to her, asking her to explain to me in English that I ought to sell him my watch. The child was frightened, she did not understand or pretended not to understand. I took advantage of this to quicken my pace and get away. But from some distance away I heard the African making a scene and calling the child and his companion to witness: 'Why, I offered him twenty shillings for his miserable watch; no one in the whole of Kigoma would make him an offer like that. But what sort of a man is he? And where would he find anyone like me? He's a silly man, a man who doesn't understand his own interest, a man as stupid as a buffalo . . .', etc.

In a very bad temper, I went back to the hotel. By now it was time for us to leave. But I heard a clamour of voices in the courtyard, the voices of my travelling companions. I went up to them and was immediately told: 'Somebody's stolen an envelope from my room with a thousand dollars in it and two hundred thousand lire, all in cash.'

'And you leave an envelope with money in it in a hotel room? Better to carry one's money in one's pocket.'

'The envelope was still there an hour ago.'

All of a sudden, from a door over which was inscribed the word 'Management', emerged the Indian with the projectile-shaped head. In a baritone voice he said: 'What do I hear? What have you come to tell me? Money has been stolen from a room in my hotel! It's not possible! My waiters are above any sort of suspicion.'

I was at once struck by the theatrical tone and style of his intervention. All at once I had become the spectator, instead of the victim, of an unpleasant affair. The man's completely false and insincere voice made it permissible to suppose the worst. But it was not as in real life, when one foresees the worst; rather as from a seat in a theatre, when one foresees, with curiosity, the development of the drama.

Meanwhile the manager was going on with his act. 'I cannot believe it! The first time in twenty years of management! I'm not just an ordinary African. I am a Pakistani, related to the Aga Khan. My honour is involved.'

'Anyhow, the money has disappeared.'

'Your affirmation grieves me. It is a blot on the reputation of the hotel. A relation of the Aga Khan cannot endure such a blot! Let us go to the room. The money will come to light.'

We went to the room, turned everything upside down: all in vain. The manager, towering to his full height, heart-broken, turned towards a small, slim, coal-black waiter with an attractive face and the beautiful, frightened eyes of a gazelle: 'Leave me alone with this man. You'll see that the money will come to light.'

Hopefully, we left the room. Five minutes went by, ten, fifteen. Someone hazarded an idea: 'He wants to make us lose time.' Then, at last, the two came out. The manager proclaimed: 'He has nothing to do with it. The only thing for you to do is to go to the police.'

'And what will the police do?'

'We have an extremely good police force. They will find the thief and the money.'

'In how long a time?'

'A week, at any rate.'

'But we have to leave in half an hour. And the train goes only three times a week.'

'If I were you, I would give up the idea of leaving and stay at Kigoma for the ten or fifteen days that the inquiries may take.'

'What? A minute ago it was a week. And now it's fifteen days?'

'Fifteen days, perhaps even twenty.'

'But do you in fact want us to go or to stay? Anyone would think that you want us to go away as quickly as possible.'

'I want you to stay. A month soon passes. After all, you have lost a thousand dollars.'

'And two hundred thousand lire.'

The play-acting continued, inflexibly. After a short consultation, we decided to leave. Whoever it was that stole the money knew what he was doing. He stole it one hour before our departure, foreseeing that in the end we should prefer to lose the money rather than stay at Kigoma. He also foresaw that we should foresee that staying at Kigoma would be useless. But as we went round looking for the manager, we found that he had disappeared. Like an actor who goes away after saying his part, he had shut himself up again in the management room. Crestfallen and full of suspicions, we followed the African servants who were laden with our baggage out of the hotel.

Our cars had only about a hundred metres to go before they stopped in front of the station. It was drizzling; and the pile of our baggage attracted dozens of frantic arms. It was the same throng, seeking a few pennies, that used to be found, barely half a century ago, at the stations of Mediterranean Europe. As usual, it was the strongest who won in this struggle for life at Kigoma. They took charge of our suitcases.

Later, we looked out of the train windows; the train was still at a standstill. Amongst the crowd, in the wet half-light, a subhuman howling suddenly broke out. A man was struggling between two guards who were gripping him by the arms. It was an unauthorized traveller who had hidden himself in the lavatory. He was howling and struggling, and, as he howled and struggled, he came undressed. He was an athletic young man; he was writhing furiously; and there he was, naked to the waist, and he left his shirt in the hands of the guards and was trying to escape. They seized hold of him again; again he started to howl; and his trousers fell down from his loins to his feet. Now he was stark naked, glossy from the rain, completely black save for the white of his eyes and of his teeth. He leapt out of the circle of people who were watching his furious strip-tease and broke free again; the last I saw of him was his muscular, powerful buttocks disappearing into the bush beyond the arched roof of the station. Essentially, he had been naked all the time; he had wanted, even without paying, to go to Dar-es-Salaam to clothe himself with our culture; he had not succeeded; he had fled, naked again, into the bush of his ancestors. Slowly the train began to move.

17

The Wedding at Tabora

Entebbe, March 1969

We had good luck at Tabora. We were wandering round the
stalls in the market which, with African indifference and
equally African passion for buying and selling, displayed
American and Australian tinned foods, bananas, sweet
potatoes, pawpaws and mangoes, when a tumult broke out
over in a corner of the square. Everyone hurried in that
direction; and we hurried there too. They told us it was a
wedding: the nuptial ceremony had already taken place,
and now the married couple and the guests were going to
the banquet which, alternating with dancing and music and
songs, would go on till late into the night. The crowd
prevented us from seeing; but by standing on the tips of
our toes we caught a fleeting glimpse of the group of
musicians in the first row who were making a deafening din
with drums and pipes and whistles. Then came a second
group composed almost exclusively of women who, it might
have been thought, were already in a state of exaltation
approaching trance: at one moment they shouted confusedly, with wild gaiety, then they chanted a doleful dirge
punctuated by an exclamatory, monotonous refrain. Finally
there was a long procession of funereal black cars with
glittering nickel-plate fittings: the married couple and the
guests. The procession passed slowly along underneath the
trees, past the sheds, the bungalows, the half-finished
houses, the quarter-finished villas, the huts of the shapeless
main road. Through the hubbub, in the blazing sunshine,
through the feverish jostling of the crowd, it wound its way
towards distant suburbs hidden by clouds of dust. I was

reminded of those lines of Rimbaud, so oriental and indeed so African:

'Un beau matin, chez un peuple fort doux, un homme et une femme superbes criaient sur la place publique: "Mes amis, je veux qu'elle soit reine!" "Je veux être reine!" Elle riait et tremblait. Il parlait aux amis de révélation, d'épreuve terminée. Ils se pâmaient l'un contre l'autre.

En effet ils furent rois toute une matinée, où les tentures carminées se relevèrent sur les maisons, et tout l'après-midi, où ils s'avancèrent du côté des jardins de palmes.'

Marvellous Rimbaud! Here, in fact, the red curtains in the windows looking on to the street were raised to afford a better view of the procession; and over there, in the distance, in the dust, rose the outlines of slender palm-trees stirred by the wind and shining in the sun. The bride and bridegroom, as in Rimbaud's lines, would be king and queen for the whole day. Tomorrow they would be absorbed again by the squalor and the torpor of the ancient African town.

We stopped in the shade of a large mango-tree, in front of what appeared to be a restaurant or an hotel. There was a dense crowd round the door. We did not manage to see the newly married pair; but we contrived to be present at the ritual exhibition of the bedroom furniture. Taken from a lorry and passing above the heads of the crowd on many upraised arms, two armchairs with purple covers, enclosed in transparent cellophane bags, travelled unsteadily towards the door of the restaurant. Cries of admiration, of jubilation and approval accompanied the hesitant transit of these two important pieces of equipment. Even before the armchairs had been swallowed up in the doorway, the transport of the mattress over the crowd began, greeted with a frenzied clamour – a double mattress covered with a blue flowered material, it also wrapped in cellophane. After the mattress, it was the turn of the two bed-ends, made of metal but painted to look like wood and incongruous in that country of forests; then the bed-springs; the bedside table; two white porcelain chamber-pots; and a 1900-style lamp in the shape of a ball. All these objects came out of the lorry, were passed, swaying and insecure, with loud cries of joy, over the heads of the crowd, and then disappeared into the doorway. Finally, out of a car and with some difficulty, there descended two enormous matrons, their big bodies swathed in brilliant-coloured materials with great floral designs, their arms bare and as thick as thighs. On round pads on the top of their heads they bore two trays of the largest size ever seen, upon which rose two mountainous packages done up in huge knotted handkerchiefs. These packages contained the pilaff of rice and mutton which no doubt would supply the main part of the nuptial banquet. The two trays, again amidst thunderous applause, were handed over the heads of the crowd and engulfed in the doorway. The party could now begin.

A white wall surrounded a small courtyard; trees with great leafy branches overhung it. Both wall and branches were laden with curious spectators who were looking down at the throng of dancers. The latter were dancing squeezed together and almost stationary for lack of space; but to make up for this they jumped up and down like puppets propelled by powerful, unaccountable springs. The composition of the band that squatted on the ground showed a compromise between the traditional and the modern: there were a number of drums but there was also a saxophone. The music, indeed, was that of American jazz; but, curiously, these rhythms, invented by American Negroes for the public dance-halls of the United States, here at Tabora, in deepest Africa, seemed to be returning to their original sources; that is to say, they revealed themselves, in some way or other, as authentically African. Perhaps because the musicians added a bizarre, archaic frenzy to them which originally they did not have; perhaps because the dancers danced them with, so to speak, a religious spirit, not as though they were ordinary, everyday tunes, which in reality they are, but the music of ritual and celebration. And, indeed, when two of my companions started dancing too, the crowd at once formed a circle round them, in a respectful, interested manner, as if faced with something foreign and never before seen; instead of which it was a question of the same dance being interpreted and performed in a different spirit.

That the spirit was religious and not merely festive was proved also by the fact that here *everybody* was dancing – contagiously, as it were – even those who took no part in the celebrations, even those who were excluded from them. They were dancing in the courtyards of the adjoining houses; they were dancing outside the restaurant, in the street. Wherever a musician squatted down on the ground and began beating the two ends of a drum with the palms of his hands, the crowd immediately formed a circle and the dancers placed their hands on one another's shoulders; and the tribal round dance started to gyrate, rhythmical, wild, like a snake biting its own tail, in the sunshine, the dust and the sweat. All these men and women were dancing for pleasure, for emotional relief, from a biological urge; but there were also professional female dancers, hired for the occasion no doubt, just as in Europe, on similar occasions, people engage waiters and masters of ceremony. These professionals remained inside a small courtyard. Now they were seated on the ground, motionless and exhausted; a little later, galvanized by the sound of the drum, they were displaying themselves in overwhelming, faultless dancing. Dressed in yellow, with yellow turbans, their age was astounding; they were wrinkled Fates the blackness of whose skin conferred upon them some infernal quality. But, on reflection, their old age was explained and justified: a religious celebration demands not so much beautiful as skilled dancers. Thus in Japan the geishas are never beautiful; but they know how to entertain guests in a professional manner.

One of the main characteristics of modern life is that one can be transported in the course of a few hours from one reality to another, from one dimension to another. Two hours earlier we were at Tabora, in a world which cannot have changed much from what it was two or three centuries ago; now, sitting in the cabin of a small passenger plane, we were already flying above Tabora in the direction of

Mwanza. From the aeroplane one could see very well why life at Tabora has aspects that are so traditional, so stagnant and so backward. Wild bush country encircles the town on all sides, thick, green and contorted. Not a town, not a house, not a sign of cultivation, not even a road. Here and there, blue and shining, the loop of a river curves briefly among the green and then disappears. Tabora was an important centre of the slave-trade until the trade was abolished; and, indeed, one can still visit, not far from Tabora, the ignoble ruins of a caravanserai where the Arab raiders allowed their human cattle to rest before sending them on to the market at Zanzibar. Tabora must have fallen into considerable decadence since the splendours brought by that trade: it has few local resources, for the most part agricultural; State aid is limited to the presence of the administrative bureaucracy; traditional culture is reduced to costume, in expectation of becoming a tourist attraction. Farewell to Tabora.

Suddenly, in the sky in front of us, appeared a small black raincloud. With sly rapidity it spread this way and that, invading the blue of the sky. Then it opened like a basket with a hole in the bottom, dropping a cataract of dull, grey rain on the still sun-lit landscape. Suddenly we were almost in darkness. Then suddenly we emerged at full speed directly over the runway which, down below us, appeared to be in a ferment of muddy water. The pilot was seeking to bring the plane down; but the speed was too great and clearly it would not be possible to land within the limit of the airfield. In fact, when within a short distance from the ground, the plane rose again, climbing abruptly and quivering and shaking along the whole span of its wings; then, like a wounded wild duck, it went staggering towards a hill. I thought we should crash against the hill; I was certain we should all be killed; and a great calm possessed me, of what I may describe as a technical kind: privately I speculated upon the capability of the engines to recover in such a short time and at such a short distance from the obstacle. The hill was getting nearer, and I saw trees the size of cabbages, meadows, dappled cows grazing on the slope.

Then – there was no knowing how – we went past. But then – a second hill; then a third. The plane started slowly banking, turning on its wing. The landscape seemed to rise and take up a vertical position as we climbed. The plane came back into a horizontal position and there was the runway. Then it sank lower, until the wheels touched the ground, and it started rolling through the water which splashed and darkened the glass of the windows. The plane came to a halt, the engines were turned off, the door was opened, and we went down into the rain, incredulous and, presumably, fortunate.

An hour later we were in the air again, in flight over Lake Victoria. The second largest lake in the world, as large as Ireland. We flew for two hours without seeing the end of it. A mirror of grey water, flat, opaque, utterly deserted, of a prehistoric, antediluvian solitude. The horizon was an arbitrary line which changed position as we went; one felt that the lake continued beyond this line, to an indefinite extent. We flew on, and some unattractive islands, of a dull green, came into view. We were flying low. On a deserted beach I saw a very long canoe, hollowed out of a single tree-trunk. Beside it were two other smaller canoes. Then I caught sight of a white rock. But as the plane drew nearer all this whiteness vanished, was scattered over the sky, and the rock became black as coal in the midst of the flat, grey water. It was a multitude of birds; they circled, all together, over the lake and then returned to the rock. We flew on.

18

Beads and Tourism

Abidjan, April 1970

In the beginning there were the small Portuguese forts at intervals along the coast, with garrisons of soldiers with iron helmets on their heads, helmets which we can see again today, strange and grotesque, in the sculptures of Benin. They were there to defend the first European arrogance: knick-knacks and beads in exchange for gold, precious stones and rare spices. But the Africans did not know that the beads were worth nothing, and the gold and precious stones a great deal. Their scale of values was that of the imagination; the European scale of values, on the other hand, was that of profit. Then, during the following two centuries, came the slave-traders, dressed in velvet and silk and brocade, in short breeches and hose, swords at their side; and again, in exchange for knick-knacks and beads, the Africans provided something precious, their brothers rounded up with the complicity and authorization of their kings and then placed in chains, embarked on ships and sold in America like cattle. This time again the Africans were ignorant of the inestimable value of the human merchandise with which they provided the Europeans in exchange for beads. But the Europeans were perfectly conscious of this value – Christianity had been teaching it to them for centuries – and thus the pretence that they were ignorant, like the Africans, that a man is not a mere thing, this was the great crime of the Europeans during those two centuries. After about twenty million persons had been sold into slavery, the slave-trade came to an end and the colonialist phase began. Once again the disparity between the European who knew the value of what he was acquiring and the non-value of what he was giving in return, coupled with the childish ignorance of the African, resolved itself into a form of violence perpetrated by the former to the detriment of the latter. Colonialism, in exchange for freedom, gave something which, there and then, was called 'civilization': that is, administrative, police and military bureaucracy, forced labour, recruitment for European wars and so on. Now we come to our own day. Colonialism is disappearing; but it is immediately followed by neo-capitalism; it is the time of so-called 'raw materials' bartered for illusory national independence; and the relationship between Europeans and Africans does not change. Violence remains, even if it is less evident. How should it be described? Let us call it an economic, touristic, cultural violence.

At this point someone may ask: but what ought it to have been, then, this relationship between Africa and Europe? My reply is: the African is not 'different' from the European, he is not 'another person'. He is simply the other face of the European, his complement, his alternative. In exploiting, enslaving, oppressing the African, the European has in reality exploited, enslaved, oppressed his 'other' self. His violence, in other words, has been a suicidal violence exercised by 'history' against his own indispensable, irreplaceable 'anti-history'. The symbol of this relationship might be, on the one hand, the helmets, the breastplates, the silks and brocades worn by the Portuguese, on the other, the innocent nakedness of the Africans. 'History' clothes itself and, as time passes, continually changes its clothes; 'anti-history' is naked and remains naked. History clothes itself and changes its clothes because, in order to exist and to develop, it needs to reject nature, that is, nudity; anti-history is nature itself, that is, nudity, stationary and outside time. The complementary nature of these two human situations requires no comment. Recognizing in the African not so much an alternative, a complement to himself as an inanimate, insignificant thing to be exploited, to be sold, to be made use of, the European has in reality, even sooner than the African, debased the natural, primitive part of himself.

I have spoken of the economic, touristic and cultural violence of today. The hotel at Abidjan, capital of the Ivory Coast Republic, where we now were, was an unwitting museum of this new violence. Built on a small hill facing the harbour, it was simply a New York skyscraper transferred, lock, stock and barrel, to this strip of Africa. The first violence lies in its proportions. The gigantic size of the hotel is not in harmony either with the town or with the country, but rather with the gigantic scale of the interests of the Western tourist industry, for which the Ivory Coast is merely one of the many sunshine and exoticism markets to which to send people from the 'metropolis' (or, as such places used to be called in the times of classic colonialism the 'mother countries') to spend their holidays. And thus we find ourselves still in a colonial 'settlement'; only, instead of being, as it was four centuries ago, a fortress armed with bronze culverins, it is an hotel with hundreds of air-conditioned rooms.

The second violence lies in the transformation of African culture into the 'boutique'. All through the vast rooms and winding passages and huge halls the thing which, half a century ago, caused one of the greatest revolutions in Western culture – the discovery of Negro art – all that was investigated, studied, understood and assimilated by restricted groups of artists and critics now appears transformed into affected decoration, at the same time both false and proud of its own falseness. It is a question of an aesthetic violence that displays, above all, obtuseness. Rather than grasp the secret of the ritual masks, they have thought it better to manufacture colossal enlargements of them and hang them on the walls to give 'colour'; rather than revive the magic of the totems, they have thought it better to use them as supporting pillars in bars and exotic restaurants; rather than penetrate the mystery of the lightning-like syntheses of the statuettes with religious or erotic themes, they have thought it better to make gigantic reproductions of them and place them in the middle of entrance-halls, the main collecting point for the luggage of recently arrived travellers. Here one is bound to admit that this neo-African decoration is often entertaining and elegant. So much the worse. It means that not only the usual popularizers but also artists, specialists and aesthetes have collaborated in the insolence of consumer society.

The third aspect of touristic violence is the isolation of the village of the African *hinterland* in contrast to the sociability of the *de luxe* hotel. It is an isolation due to the lack of roads and of means of communication. The hotel has no relationship with Africa; it has a relationship only with the West, of which it is both an emanation and an outpost. It takes five hours to fly from Paris to the hotel; but it is often impossible to reach villages not more than about a hundred kilometres from Abidjan. The narrow network of connections between the hotel and Rome, Paris, London and New York is, on consideration, the cause of the complete lack of connection between the hotel and the village.

I recall an expedition to one of these villages that are so near and at the same time so difficult of access. We went by car, along a rough, red track through the equatorial forest towards the frontier with Ghana. Then from the car we transferred to a motor-boat. In the Ivory Coast a number of lagoons, so straight and motionless and regular that they look like big canals, stretch for hundreds of kilometres, parallel with the sea, through the sand-dunes and the bush. The motor-boat travelled on for hours and hours without the slightest change in the landscape; and this is a typically African characteristic: monotony or, if you prefer it, repetition *ad infinitum* of a single motif, a single detail. At last, at the far end of the lagoon, beyond a narrow passage between two high dunes, we saw the glistening boisterous foam of breakers in the open sea. We had reached the coast. Here, on one bank of the lagoon, a hut awaited us, a hut *de luxe* on sham piles, where later, to the sound of the radio, we should eat food cooked according to the best Parisian recipes; on the other bank was a village, a village, it appeared, of the most authentic, untouched kind. We went to look at this village. Shaded by a grove of tall, slender palm-trees, the huts, of dark, seasoned wood, were reminiscent of huts in the Alps. All were surrounded by fences inside which hens were scratching about, pigs were wallowing, and naked children with prominent navels staggered as they walked; all had a pile of coconuts in front of their doors. The village was deserted because the fishing-boats were on the point of coming in from the ocean, and this was a great social event in the almost complete isolation of the little community. On the beach women, old men and children were lined up along the backwash. As the long prows of the canoes came into view above the waves, a hilarious, excited animation spread from one face to another. Then the boats slid on to the beach and were hauled up on dry land.

While the little crowd rushed laughing and shouting towards the fishermen, I noticed a singular fact. We were three Europeans; the village, as I have already mentioned, was isolated among its sand-dunes, with scarcely any possibility of communicating with the rest of the world; nevertheless these men and women, who would have been justified in considering us complete strangers, exerted themselves to make us share in their festivity. They smiled, pointed out the boats to us, took the fish and showed them to us; they wished, in fact, that we should be merry in their company. I could not help comparing this welcoming attitude with the completely opposite attitude that would have been taken up, on a similar occasion, by the Indians of Bolivia among whom I had found myself three weeks earlier. And I understood the reason for this difference. The Indians have had something resembling a history, and then the Spaniards interrupted and destroyed it and the Indians have never forgotten this, and still today they consider the Spaniards as usurpers and maintain a kind of unconscious social rejection towards them. As for the Africans, they, on the other hand, have known only anti-history, that is, nature, which, itself too strong to be dominated, has in turn dominated them, outside any sort of history. They have suffered, perhaps, more than the Indians, being

107

exploited, enslaved, oppressed; but, unlike the Indians, they have forgotten, or at most remember the tragedies of the past as they remember natural calamities, without historical rancour but with a serenity which, in the end, becomes forgetfulness.

I thought of these things as I watched the lively, joyous crowd round the fishing-boats. The fish was now on the ground, and some women were already scraping off the scales with knives. Then I felt a small hand thrust firmly into mine. It was the hand of a little boy of perhaps four years old, completely naked except for a string of blue beads round his waist and passing between his legs to serve as a loincloth. He was another one who had forgotten, who bore no grudge, who lived in anti-history. Smiling, he said to me: '*Moi et toi, camarade.*'

19

Desert, Prairie, Forest

Bamako, April 1970

One evening at Bamako we were present at an exhibition
of national dances organized by the authorities in a local
night-club. A large part of the *corps diplomatique* was there
and a number of official personages. On the cement floor,
lit by floodlights, there was a succession of *corps de ballet*
in African costumes, pairs of flute-players and trios of
drummers. In a similar dance-hall in Europe these dances
and this music would have seemed authentic. And not only
because of the violence, the strangeness and the queer
harmony of gestures and voices and sounds, but also
because of the not very professional enthusiasm of the
dancers and players. In Africa, beneath the fiercely sparkling starlight, in the coolness of a slight wind laden with
savage odours and seeming to come straight from the
prairie, one felt, on the other hand, that the authenticity
of the dances and the music had already, from the point of
view of folk-lore, undergone alteration and mitigation.
They were dances and music that had originally been
performed in the villages on ritual and propitiatory occasions. Here, on the contrary, the occasion was social and
arranged as a tourist attraction. In the villages the voices
would have been harsher and more discordant, the convulsions of the dance more strongly rhythmical and more
violent, the music more monotonous, more hallucinatory.

And then there would have been something that we
remember noticing in dances of the same kind, some years
ago, in a village in Ghana: the feeling of being present at an
event which 'ignored' us, which 'excluded' us, which had no

need of our presence and derived its own *raison d'être* from motives that did not concern us. At Bamako, on the other hand, it was on our presence that the event depended. And instead of 'excluding' us, the performers sought to implicate us by arousing our curiosity and stimulating our admiration.

Strange to say, this decline in African authenticity is due, fundamentally, to the justification, on a political and cultural level, of that same authenticity – that is to say, to nationalism. While I was in Bolivia, a short time before going to Africa, I read the following remarks in a letter from Régis Debray, the French revolutionary imprisoned at Camiri: 'The nation is the essential element of these times and no one should believe a single word of any kind of socialism that does not also contain nationalism . . . There will never be an authentic nation on this continent without a revolutionary socialism, just as there will never be a socialism without a revolutionary nationalism.'

The phenomenon to which Debray alludes has been known now for nearly two centuries, that is, from the time of the French Revolution which marked its beginning. It is the explosive partnership of national feeling with the universalized ideology of the moment. In the nineteenth century the partnership was between national feeling and liberal ideology; today it is, or ought to be, between national feeling and socialist ideology. Debray was speaking of Latin America, but his argument might also hold good for Africa. After all, the history of Africa is not so very different from that of Latin America. Both these continents are areas of depression and under-development. Both have experienced colonialism and liberation (real or counterfeit) from colonialism. I have said that Debray's argument might also hold good for Africa; but in reality there are strong probabilities that, on the contrary, it will not hold good.

Why is this so? Because nationalism, wherever it develops, in symbiosis, as we have said, with the universalized ideology of the moment, thrusts its roots down into the soil of history. At the source of the socialist nationalism, for instance, of the Arab countries or of the countries of Eastern Asia, there is the history of the Arab people, of the Chinese people, of the Vietnamese people. In Latin America, too, at the source of the nationalism hoped for by Debray, apart from the history of four centuries of Spanish culture transplanted into the New World, there is the history of the very many preceding centuries of pre-Columbian culture. But in Africa the tribal culture which preceded colonialism had no truly historical characteristic features: there, we still find ourselves not so much in history as in prehistory. Furthermore, African nationalism cannot count upon the transplantation into Africa of an ancient European culture, as in Latin America. Colonialism in Africa, moreover, has lasted for three centuries less than in Latin America; besides, it is not a colonialism for purposes of population but of mere exploitation. People went to Latin America in order to stay there; they went to Africa to enrich themselves and then go back home. Even colonialism, in fact, does not make history in Africa, it is merely a chapter in European history. But then, since there is a lack of history of any kind whatever, from whence should the African nationalism of tomorrow derive its starting-point?

Now the paradox is that, although it had no terrain adapted to nationalism, Black Africa has been, so to speak, anxious to invent one for itself, inasmuch as the nations do exist. Take for example French West Africa. The entirely 'non-historical' alternations of this vast region are very simple. Before the French intervention there was merely the flattest, the lowest, the most arid part of the African continent. A 'situation', therefore, in no way historical but natural, the character of which was determined by the alternation of the three great climatic bands which cross Africa from west to east, from the Atlantic to the Red Sea: desert, prairie and forest. The tribes which in thousands, with thousands of dialects, religions, usages and customs, peopled this region, as limitless as it is uniform, constituted, by their number and their variety, the other, contradictory aspect of the natural simplicity and monotony. In other words, there was tribal anarchy just as there was geographical unity.

Then the French arrived and this, so to speak, prehistoric

111

state of affairs came to an end; but this did not mean that history had really begun. The great body of Africa was stretched out on the operating-table of the European Imperialist congresses and was dissected. A piece of Africa fell to the lot of each of the European nations (according to European criteria). Then France took to pieces its own piece, French West Africa, and called the pieces colonies. The colony of Senegal, of French Guinea, of the Ivory Coast, of Dahomey, of the French Sudan, of the Upper Volta, of Mauritania, of the Niger. Eight pieces, that is, eight colonies.

It was the year 1895. The period of the colonies, that is, of the eight pieces of Africa, which meant nothing to the Africans who were still tied to their tribal culture and to the economy of desert and prairie and forest but had, on the other hand, a very precise meaning for the colonialists, lasted for barely seventy years. About 1960 or thereabouts, French West Africa became 'independent' and the 'colonies', all of a sudden, became 'nations'. The nation of Mali, the nation of Senegal, the nation of Mauritania, the nation of the Ivory Coast, the nation of the Upper Volta, the nation of Guinea, the nation of the Niger. But at the starting-point of these nations there was and still is – an incontestable, indestructible reality – the immense stretch of territory, so simple (desert, prairie, forest) and at the same time so complicated (the thousands of tribes), which existed before the colonialist invasion. And thus, by a typically African paradox, the independence and the transformation of the colonies into nations has led, for lack of historical roots, to the creation of a nationalism which is so only in name but not in fact – the nationalism of the African administrative personnel which has everywhere supplanted the European administrative personnel, without however affecting (with the exception of the Guinea of Sekou Touré) the European interests, becoming, in fact, their legitimate representative. Hence various consequences – amongst many others, the metamorphosis of African culture into folk-lore for tourists.

The day following the display of dance and music in the night-club, we made a tour of the town of Bamako. We saw the quarters in which are situated the bungalows and suburban villas once inhabited by the French administrators and in which the new African middle class is now installed. It is a middle class that speaks perfect French, that lives in houses with furniture actually of the Swedish type, with all the necessary household electrical appliances and, on the walls, reproductions of pictures of the *école de Paris*. But this middle class has its roots not in Bamako, once a French settlement and now the bureaucratic capital; but rather in the villages where people continue to live in the traditional manner, in an atmosphere not exactly nationalist but, so to speak, 'sub-African', according to the laws and the culture of the desert, the prairie and the forest.

After our walk round the town, we went by car up a small hill, the only one in the limitless plain that surrounds Bamako on every side. We stopped the car at a bare patch of rust-red ground and looked down at the panorama of Bamako. The town looked like an attenuated whitish design in an immense, uniformly green carpet. Here, on the two shores of the very wide, lazy, transparent Niger, the Europeans embroidered the geometrical pattern of the town, with its straight streets crossing at right angles, on to the limitless green fabric of the plain. But the plain all round the town stretches away, unrelieved, in all directions, beyond, far beyond the political and 'national' frontiers of Mali, unreal because of its vastness and its monotony but perhaps, just because it is so unreal, the only real thing in this part of the world. Above this limitless plain is the sky of Africa, pale blue: it too of an unreal vastness, with its horizons dimmed by the sultry heat and its wandering white clouds.

The immensity of the sky, the immensity of the plain seem to form an alliance to make the small, regular white patch of Bamako's built-up area insignificant and almost invisible. The future of Africa lies probably in the conflict between the size and uniformity of its nature and the arbitrary artificiality of the nations that have been cut out of it. It may be that from this conflict there will truly begin, tomorrow, the history of Africa.

20

Timbuktu

Timbuktu, May 1970

In Africa the aeroplane is more revealing than the car
because Africa is monotonous and repetitious and from a
plane this monotony and repetition can be contemplated
whereas in a car they have to be endured. The prairie, for
example, which is monotony and repetition *par excellence*
with its millions of acacias on millions of sandy dunes, can
be better comprehended in all its utter wildness from the
sky than from the road. Next we had a sight of one of those
endless marshes in which inland waters in Africa collect and
stagnate. In this case it was a question of the marsh
formed by the inability, so to speak, of the River Niger to
take a proper shape, at the most northerly point of its great
loop. We flew over this Niger marsh for nearly an hour
without ever seeing the end of it. It was of a pale, diaphanous
blue, subdivided by tongues and isthmuses of land of a pale
green, into a number of minor basins, pools, canals, floods,
lakes and fens. It was an amphibious world and one could
see very well from the plane that the land and the water
had no precise boundaries. From time to time it was possible
to distinguish, at the extreme point of a tongue of greenish
land, a small brown spot – a village. And so, after an
hour's flight over the watery heart of Africa, we arrived at
Timbuktu.

Certainly it is a grand, or rather, a glamorous name (for
in reality no historical event has ever taken place there,
unless the feuds between the two tribes of the Fulbé and
the Tuareg can be called historical); but now it is nothing
more than a name. A caravan town, of the type illustrated

by Rostovtsev in his study on Palmyra, Timbuktu once despatched and received caravans from Tunisia, Algeria, Morocco, the Ivory Coast, Nigeria. Nowadays merchandise goes by sea and the Timbuktu caravans are reduced to groups of camels transporting slabs of rock salt looking like pink marble, excavated by the convicts of Mali in a mine in the middle of the Sahara, a thousand kilometres from the town. Timbuktu, in short, is a town of not more than fifteen thousand inhabitants. With a future for the tourist industry, possibly, but nothing more.

We drove round Timbuktu by car and saw the whole place in little more than half an hour, in spite of the efforts of our patriotic guide who would have liked to extend this half-hour into two or three hours. And what is there to see at Timbuktu? A modern monument to Independence; a house with a plaque recording the French explorer Caillé who stayed there in 1828, the first after the almost legendary Ibn-Batuta; a small market on the bank of the Niger; the usual administrative buildings. And then, lastly, the mosque.

Smaller than those of Djenné and Mopti, the mosque nevertheless confers a title of nobility upon the sleepy African town whose dull, empty streets, invaded by the sand of the neighbouring desert, lack even the traditional shops which elsewhere go to indicate, at least, the antiquity of local craftsmanship. The mosque does in fact testify that the town actually forms part of the ancient, fascinating Sudanese culture which is so similar to the prairie of which it is the direct expression. The prairie is the symbiosis of the bush and the desert; the Sudan has been and still is, the symbiosis of the pastoral, Mohammedan Arab world with the peasant, animist Negro world. It is easier to 'feel' than to analyse the fascination of the historical Sudan. With considerable simplification, it can be said that it consists in the adoption on the part of the Africans, peaceful, sedentary but primitive agriculturists, of an errant, military religion like Islam which, instead of combating their primitiveness (as Christianity has done and is still doing), appears instead to have aimed, for its own ends, at liberating and unleashing it. Islam has changed the Negroes of the Sudan from a community-type, patriarchal society into a different society, feudal and relatively more modern. At the same time it has replaced the obscure terrors of animism by the impetuosity of monotheistic fanaticism.

The Sudanese mosque at Timbuktu is the architectural illustration of this metamorphosis of 'negritude' in the direction of Mohammedanism. 'Sudan' comes from the Arab term *Bilad al-sud an,* which means 'land of the Negroes'; but the mosque immediately gives one to understand that it is a question of a radically Islamized 'land of the Negroes'. In this building there is nothing 'naturistic', magical, or demoniacal, as in the huts of the witch-doctors in the equatorial forests; nor is there anything mystical, cultural, or refined, as in the mosques of Morocco and Egypt. The mosque at Timbuktu looks like a barbarian fortress. And this fortress is not made of stone or bricks but of sunbaked clay, the kind of clay that the French call *pisé* and the Spaniards *adobe.* And it is the humblest material in existence; it is used by the underdeveloped peoples of the arid zone of the globe: Persia, Turkey, Mexico, the Sudan, Arabia. But it is a very expressive material.

What is it that *adobe* expresses? Humility, indigence; but also a certain unadaptability, a certain boldness; and, in the largest buildings, as, for instance, in the Sudanese mosques, a barbaric aggressiveness, a fanatical bellicosity. In other words, to be precise, the Negro primitiveness freed from animism and exalted by Islamic fanaticism.

Like a fortress, as we have said, the mosque has battlemented walls and, at its four corners, instead of slender minarets, four squat conical towers. What gives the building its barbaric character is the decorative element of a number of large black spikes sticking out of the walls and the towers like the quills of a porcupine. These are simply the ends of the beams that form the structure of the building; but projecting as they do into the air, sharp and black against the light background of the clay, they give the mosque an indescribably military, threatening appearance, not in the least religious in the sense of contemplative devotion. This impression, moreover, is confirmed by the cavernous, dusty bareness of the rooms, the staircases and the corridors. The Sudanese mosque is, in reality, typified here, in these battlemented walls, in these towers bristling with spikes. But one is forced to admire the evocative power of art, even when rough and inarticulate as it is in this mosque. At the mere sight of these towers, memories at once came to mind of Negro kings and warriors of Islam whom the Europeans encountered in the past, both in war and peace. Of these potentates a record has remained even in the burlesque catalogues in Don Quixote and the Orlando Furioso. Today they survive in the still feudal constructions of the society of the prairie.

After our tour of Timbuktu, we returned to the hotel and went and sat on the terrace. Facing us was a corner of Sudanese Africa, minute but complete. The Niger at that point formed a pleasant little lake. On its banks were tall, slanting, ruffled palm-trees. Behind the palms rose the dunes of the desert. Upon the dunes squatted an entire herd of camels. Then, in this motionless picture, suddenly everything moved. The camels rose up one after another and went down to the lake to drink. They stretched out their necks to the water, or else raised their muzzles and gave forth long, raucous cries. At the same moment something happened on the terrace as well. A troupe of three Parisian models and a couple of photographers were preparing to portray the latest summer fashions against the background of the lake, the palm-trees, the dunes and the camels. The girls arranged themselves in the comic attitudes of challenge which nowadays are obligatory in such exhibitions. The photographers took their pictures in a great hurry, fearful that the camels might go away.

These photographs would be published in Europe in glossy fashion magazines, and certainly someone, seeing them, would think: 'How far can technical skill go? They reconstruct a corner of Africa in order to launch a few rags!' But that was not so. No corner of Africa was reconstructed. The models had merely arrived in Timbuktu, after five hours' flight from Paris, and made use of

117

Timbuktu as a ready-made corner of Africa. Timbuktu, in short, had been 'consumed'. The word 'consumer', as we know, is a commonplace nowadays. But that was precisely what the models had come to seek in Timbuktu: a commonplace.

21

Tuareg for Tourists

Timbuktu, May 1970

We went to a Tuareg encampment about a hundred kilometres from Timbuktu. There was no road, of course, merely a track. We travelled at thirty kilometres an hour, keeping to the deep ruts made in the sand by preceding cars. We travelled but seemed to be standing still, since the landscape does not change however much one travels. On all sides there was the same view – sand-dunes, low, bristling shrubs, thinly scattered thorny acacias with umbrella-shaped foliage. No wild animals, no camels or sheep or goats. The bush, however far one looked, was empty. And yet everywhere there could be seen the black, dead embers of camp-fires, the excrement of camels and sheep. Where had they gone, these animals and the men who accompanied them? No one knows, the plain gives no answer to such questions.

We continued for some time along the track, and then the driver, a young Negro with a false look of thoughtfulness, left the track and launched off diagonally through the bush. Up and down we went over the dunes, avoiding the acacias by a narrow margin and plunging with perilous impetuosity into the midst of the shrubs. Actually we were going more slowly than before; but with a violence that produced an illusion of speed.

After a couple of hours of this obstacle race, the eye, dazzled by the intense, dusty light, was able to distinguish a first change: the dunes became barer, the trees and shrubs more thinly scattered; the desert was beginning to prevail over the bush. Then, at a bend in the track, we saw a rectangular hovel at its edge; on the threshold stood a man in uniform, a pistol in his belt: it was a police post. Then the dunes again, now almost without any trees. And finally, from the top of a sand-hill, the Tuareg encampment.

Vaguely circular in shape, it lay at the bottom of a broad valley of white sand. The tents were placed at the edges of the valley, forming a central space like the piazza in a village. They were dark, hairy tents made from the skins of camels and sheep irregularly sewn together. Almost every tent had an enclosure with a low fence round it, and inside the enclosure were to be seen women cooking, or the domestic animals of the Tuareg, hens, sheep, goats, asses. The open space in the middle, on the other hand, appeared to be a meeting-place, for games or for trading. Grave, proud-looking personages wrapped in dark-blue mantles, their faces entirely covered save for the slits in front of their eyes, were walking there in a dignified manner in groups of three or four; women, also swathed in blue, were carrying on animated discussions in other groups; children were chasing one another and fighting on the sand. Our arrival, however, produced a significant change in this quiet camp life.

The children stopped chasing each other and surrounded us, offering us little leather bags or cases. The women also came up to us and pulled out of the pockets of their skirts necklaces, bracelets, trinkets or daggers of local craftsmanship. As for the men, there was no change in their attitude; they went on walking, dignified and proud, but with a new shade of meaning in their gravity, a nuance intended to appeal, let us say, to the 'consumer': they too, in fact, were preparing to sell something to the tourists. Not trinkets or bags but their own picturesque image as mysterious desert warriors.

'Atlantis'! Suddenly there came to mind the memory of Pabst's film, in the thirties, with Brigitte Helm in the part of Antinea, Queen of the Sahara. The myth of the mysterious Sahara, linked with that of the no less mysterious Tuareg culture, had already at that time become a commonplace, so much so that it was possible to make a successful film out of it. In *Atlantis* Pabst transported the spectator from the luxurious caves of Antinea to the legs of French can-can dancers in a Parisian variety theatre. He moved at one bound from European civilization to the civilization that was imagined to be hidden in the solitudes of the Sahara. The Tuareg were supposed to be the archaic, warlike custodians of this civilization. The myth of Atlantis was then nothing but a story to amuse the cinema crowds; but, like all myths, it contained an allusion to something real that has nowadays been accurately proved. In the part of the Sahara which belongs to the republic of the Niger it seems that uranium mines have been discovered.

Already the French have built model villages for technicians and workmen; already an airline connects Paris with these villages. So Antinea, after all, truly existed; but in the form of a valuable mineral which is indispensable for atomic weaponry. And the Tuareg? In the myth, they were the rough skin of an exquisite fruit; by their intransigent backwardness they guaranteed the isolation of Atlantis. But today, in the mediocre reality – science-fictional though it may be – of a thermonuclear Sahara, it seems that they are bound to be gradually thrust back to the margin of history, in situations analogous to those of the Indian tribes of the great American reserves. As always, then, the real blow to the myth of the Sahara has been an economic blow. First there was the end of the camel as a means of transport, its reduction to an animal for producing milk, meat and leather. And now, with the uranium mines, the same thing will happen in the Sahara as in the deserts of the United States: two steps from the Indian tents, atomic power-stations.

In the meantime, however, the Tuareg continue to dream of a desert culture of archaic type as though the world were still the world of Ibn-Batuta. I looked at them as they crowded round us offering us the products of their leisurely craftsmanship. They all had a great beauty and purity of feature. Dark, with lineaments of Caucasian type, black eyes with clear, motionless pupils that look like obsidian, fine noses with curving nostrils and tips slightly hooked, proud mouths. They were not very insistent, in any case, with their offerings; it might have been thought they were doing it as a pastime; some of them were inattentive and began talking amongst themselves, or following us in a tired sort of way, without asking for anything. Obviously we were dealing with people who were fundamentally lazy and indifferent.

Who, then, did the work in the encampment? Here again the archaic quality of the Tuareg became apparent, for they still entrust all the domestic work to ex-slaves or descendants of slaves. The slaves, in their turn, belong to Negro tribes which from time immemorial have lived in symbiosis with the Tuareg. I use the word 'symbiosis' rather than 'servitude' because the biological term seems to me more fitting than the sociological to describe the relationship between the Tuareg and their Negro servants. And there the servants were, at work in the enclosure of one of the tents. There were three woolly-haired women with coal-black faces, very broad noses and enormous lips. Bare to the waist, with a piece of material tied round their hips, their appearance was utterly different from that of their Tuareg mistresses who were muffled up to the eyes. Gripping long pestles in their outstretched arms, they were vigorously pounding, in a big wooden tub, some kind of mush of cereals to be served at the Tuaregs' meal. They willingly allowed themselves to be photographed, continuing with their pounding but turning their laughing faces towards us and looking at us without shame. They appeared (and I dare say perhaps are) happy in their state of servility.

And the camels? The camels were not there; they were grazing somewhere or other, away from the encampment. There was one, however, for such tourists as wished to mount the so-called 'ship of the desert'. And so, one at a time, my companions climbed up on to the wooden saddle; then the camel rose time after time, uttering long, harsh cries, in protest against tourism, perhaps; finally, resigned, it would take a turn round the encampment. But the Tuaregs have a well-developed sense of humour. The last of us to mount the camel was a very fat man, and then I saw the camel-driver stealthily untie the straps of the saddle underneath the belly of the camel. The camel got up forelegs first; the saddle slipped; the tourist fell off the saddle and found himself sitting astride with his nose against the back of the animal's neck. General laughter among the Tuareg who had been waiting, perhaps since the beginning of our visit, for this joke on the part of the camel-driver.

As we went back it was already dusk; and the driver with the thoughtful expression again started off across the dunes. All at once we found ourselves in a region of thick bush with no further sign of a track. The car went up and down over the dunes, clambering with difficulty over shrubs and plants, tearing branches from trees as it passed. Then suddenly there was a sinister little lake, of a blue that was almost black, in which the red light of the sunset was already fading. We turned back, came up against a group of acacias, skirted it, and then encountered another lake. Clear spaces in the bush gave the impression of tracks that did not really exist; the dunes and thickets and shrubs were all exactly alike; the lakes multiplied maliciously. In short, we were lost; and now our car was rushing hither and thither, without any precise direction, like a cockroach gone mad.

Then, far away, we saw the figure of a passer-by, walking slowly, supported on a long stick. As it came nearer to us, we saw that it was an old woman. Naked to the waist, she had a head like a man and a face shrunken into a grotesque grimace of ancient suffering. Her breasts hung down to her waist, flattened and stretched out so that they resembled a pair of empty gloves – of those long gloves that come up to the elbow. We asked her if she wished to get into the car; she refused, but asked for something to drink. The driver handed her a big bottle of three litres' capacity; the Negress raised it to her mouth and, for five minutes on end, drank without stopping. I have never seen anyone drink so much; the old woman evidently, was exhausted, and was doing as a camel does, which fills itself with water, the fuel of the desert, before starting on a journey. She handed back the empty bottle, pointed out the right road to us and went away.

We reached the track almost immediately, but here a new surprise awaited us. The car slowed down and stopped: there was no water left in the radiator. Our driver was embarrassed; we learned that the entire supply of water for the car was contained in that large bottle which had just been emptied by the thirsty Negress. So we were brought to a halt again, in the spectral moonlight which made the bones of an ass show up white on the sand, an ass that perhaps had died of thirst in that solitary place. We waited for two hours; finally the pale apparition of our guide became visible, away among the trees and bushes, triumphantly waving the big bottle which he had gone to refill at a well used by nomads. We started off again. After barely a kilometre we saw the scattered, dim lights of Timbuktu. In the false perspective of the plain we had thougth we were still about thirty kilometres away; instead, we were only a few hundred metres from the town.

22

Baobabs Like Human Beings

Bandiagara, June 1970

Why is it that for the European in Africa the baobab-tree provides an object of continual, insatiable, contemplative wonder? Probably because European civilization is (or at least has been) strongly anthropocentric and anthropomorphic, and the baobab, amongst all the trees in the world, is without doubt the most human. I looked at them as I drove across the great plain where ‚one might almost say, they live. Here in the first row were three of them, strange upside-down trees, with huge, stout-limbed roots like branches and thin, bald branches like roots; with multiple trunks which look like bunches of trunks tied together. Behind these first three, there were six more in a second row, twelve in a third row, and then innumerable others, as far as the eye could reach, spreading over the limitless plain that pullulated with low shrubs. Like human beings, they were numerous yet solitary, gesticulating yet motionless. In common with man they also have lower extremities larger than their upper extremities, and bark that looks like smooth, fatty, elastic human skin. But above all it is their expressiveness, and one might almost say their mobility, that are human: hastening with long steps from the farthest horizons, these vegetable monsters seem to be waving their arms as they walk towards us.

Why have I wished to emphasize the 'humanity' of the baobab? Because, when we turned off the main track into a secondary trail we entered the country of the Dogoni, a small people of anthropomorphic beliefs, who have become celebrated and positively fashionable since the studies devoted to them by ethnologists during the last thirty years. The humanity of the baobab-trees served therefore as a kind of introduction to the anthropomorphism of the Dogoni cosmogony.

On the map, the names of the Western-type nations created in the post-colonial era, each one with its flag, its capital, its boundaries – Mali, Nigeria, Senegal, Upper Volta, Ghana, etc. – are written in block capitals, in heavy type, as much as to say: 'These are the names that count.' On the other hand the names of the African peoples – the Mossi, the Tuareg, the Bambara, the Paulh, the Malinké, the Minianka, and so on – are written in light, volatile italics, as much as to say: 'We give these names for exactness of information; but they do not count.' Now the opposite is true. The post-colonial African nations, at any rate for the moment, are much less 'real' than the peoples, the tribes, the ethnic groups who themselves have something much more concrete than a flag created at a desk in order to distinguish one from the other. As in the times of Herodotus, in Africa one does in fact still today travel through varying cosmogonies. And what distinguishes the peoples one from another, apart from their economic, linguistic and racial peculiarities, etc., is their explanations and conceptions of the world. Now the Dogoni, a small people (about three hundred thousand) almost submerged by the tide of Mohammedanism, are distinguished from their neighbours especially, in fact uniquely, by their notion of the cosmos based on the strangely European, Mediterranean and Christian idea that God, the world and the universe have human appearances, structures and forms.

Let us take a look at the country of the Dogoni, since we have already been crossing it for at least an hour. Let us see whether the physical aspect of the country in some way justifies such original beliefs. After all, it is not without reason that the desert, region of solitude and silence, should be Mohammedan; it is right that the sunlit, temperate Mediterranean should have been first pagan and then Catholic; logical that the Shamans should wander amongst the snows and the winds of the extreme north; and no less logical that India, unreal and suffering, should have been the land of the first Buddhism. And now the motion of the car as it advanced jolting up and down over the clefts in the stony track showed us that the Dogoni country bears a strong resemblance to the Thebaids depicted with surprising verisimilitude and precision in the paintings of the Primitives. As in the Thebaids, the ground does not consist of soil but of slabs or layers or flakes of dark grey sandstone; a surface of ground that, even though uneven and irregular, looks like a pavement.

The soil, when there is any, is to be seen in holes or wells, in basins or cracks in this pavement; in the former grow the trees, for the most part baobab; in the latter the Dogoni, admirable gardeners, grow their vegetables with expert skill and according to agricultural techniques that are in themselves anthropomorphic. These natural pavements made of great sandstone slabs are irregularly bounded here and there and, as it were, enclosed by bastions of rock which, especially from a distance, composed as they are of enormous stones and rounded masses, look like man-made ramparts, with towers, buttresses and battlements amongst which the openings of numerous caves suggest so many doors and windows. We were, in fact, in a landscape like that of the Carso in north-eastern Italy, but with a very decided 'form' of its own, a 'form' (to put it briefly) that is 'human', that is, architectural. Thus, gradually, the idea suggested itself that the Dogoni lived in a landscape made like a house or a castle or some other kind of building intended for human habitation.

We continued on our journey. The path twisted about amongst sugarloaf rocks looking like fingers or noses, circled round smooth, rotund boulders resembling breasts or buttocks, climbed over blocks of stone lying flat in which it was not difficult to recognize outlines of supine bodies, passed below sandstone slabs like dark, threatening faces with hollow eyes and screaming mouths. So the landscape, too, was anthropomorphic. Or was this an idea suggested by recent readings about the people who inhabited it?

Finally, at a bend in the track, we saw our first Dogoni.

There were five or six boys, their bodies squeezed into sacks of yellowish hempen cloth, their faces painted white; standing amongst the shrubs they were waving things like castanets. It was explained to me that the boys dressed and painted in this way had been recently initiated with the rite of circumcision. This rite of initiation means that they have to wander for some little time over the plain. They seemed cheerful and somewhat astonished at themselves. They produced the same demure, embarrassed appearance as, with us, is to be seen in boys and girls immediately after their first communion.

We greeted them, they answered us with broad smiles and a redoubled sound of castanets, and we went on our way. We came to a fabulous river (the land of the Dogoni is, fundamentally, a land of fable; and indeed in fables, in an anthropomorphic way, objects, flowers, trees and animals 'speak'), a river deeply set beneath a long rocky cliff, a river of black, still water upon which floated great white flowers and enormous green leaves. There was a hump-backed bridge without any parapet, and Dogoni women, bare to the waist, heads held erect beneath the weight of their baskets, their bosoms outlined against the empty air, like walking caryatids, stood out distinctly for a moment on the highest point of the bridge in the brilliance of the midday light, then went down on the other side and disappeared. The sunlight was violent but, strangely, it did not nullify the colours, which were clear and shrill, with a disconcerting artificial brilliance, like a film in Technicolor.

At last we reached Sangha, the goal of our journey. It is a village that has become famous owing to the ethnological and linguistic studies devoted to it by Marcel Griaule and Geneviève Calame Griaule. If we did not know that the Dogoni were anthropomorphic and that anything they invent or do always has man as its point of departure and model, we might very well mistake Sangha for any ordinary African village (given that any ordinary villages exist in Africa or elsewhere). There was the earthy open space, of an oblong oval shape, which served as the village square. There were the baobabs, monstrous and gesticulating as usual, with fruits like wasps' nests hanging from their rickety little branches: here they fulfilled the function that the more modest plane-trees have in our own squares. Then, at the two sides of the open space, were the dusty crags on the top of which, crooked and close together, were perched the huts with their circular walls and square roofs, made of rough, yellowish dried mud and devoid of windows, like dovecots.

As has been said, it looked like any ordinary village; actually it was constructed on the same symbolic principles that were the origin of the design of the Christian basilicas. These latter were built on a plan like a cross; the village has a plan like a man, who evidently, however, is a hermaphrodite, that is, he combines the characteristics of both sexes. The head is at one end, the feet at the other. In the middle, quite correctly, are to be found the hands and the male sex on one side, the female on the other. Slightly below the upper end (the head) is, naturally, the chest. Head, feet, chest, hands, sexes are specified buildings with particular functions. The Dogoni village, therefore, instead of being the result of rational calculations like villages that are built nowadays, is the outcome of a deliberation of a symbolic kind. Symbolic thought, always in search of the absolute, has thus allowed the building of an 'absolute' village, that is, a village directly linked with cosmogony. As regards the Dogoni cosmogony, it is 'absolute' because, obviously, it was, in its time, 'revealed'.

23

The World is Crockery

Bandiagara, July 1970

I looked out between two enormous boulders, on the edge of an abyss. In front of me a rocky reef stood out in the distance, like a high cliff hanging vertically over the sea, full of promontories and inlets, until, gradually diminishing but still imposing, it was lost in the heat mists of the horizon. But it was not the sea that stretched away below the cliff but the infinite blue-green expanse of the great prairie. This cliff marks the line at which the Dogoni came to a stop, when, who knows how many centuries ago, they spread over the Bandiagara massif, that strange shelf of rock which, on the plain, rises abruptly from the plain. The Dogoni were certainly few in number, possibly a few thousands, and their geographical and demographical expansion must have been extremely slow: today they inhabit the whole of the shelf of rock and there are about three hundred thousand of them. Emboldened by the inaccessibility of the region, they determined to excavate flights of steps and passages in the reef and to go down into the plain below. But they did not have the courage to go far from their natural bastion.

By leaning forward I could in fact see a Dogoni village far below, at the bottom of the overhanging cliff; but clinging to the slope under the cliff, with its yellow roofs like a cluster of mushrooms, as though fearful of the immense plain spreading away in front of it. Without doubt, this village was built according to the principles of the Dogoni cosmogony: the roofs were square because they symbolized the sky; the bases of the huts were round because they symbolized the sun. But, seen from above, the village merely looks like any other simple, poor, in no way symbolical village of African peasants. Perched high above, I gazed, fascinated, at the village, wondering why it was that the Dogoni and, in general, all peoples in their primitive phase evolve a mythical explanation of the world. The answer is not easy, it is, in fact, impossible.

The explanation of the world does not indeed usually interest or implicate anyone except those who administer it, defend it or who have originally revealed and institutionalized it: priests, witch-doctors, wise men and so on. Ordinary men, Dogoni or otherwise, content themselves with knowing that this explanation exists and is ready at hand for the time when they need it; and, for the rest, they live according to their own senses and their own modest, everyday preoccupations. This holds good for the anthropomorphic cosmogony of the Dogoni as also for that of the Bible. Why, then, an explanation of the world? Evidently for mysterious reasons, understanding by 'mysterious' everything that is not practical and utilitarian and that is related, in some way, to the imagination. It is a fact, however, that their beliefs distinguish and characterize men more than anything else, more than racial characteristics, or than their mode of behaviour, or than their occupations and trades.

As I reflected on these matters, I turned round and saw that, while I had been looking out from the top of the precipice, a number of boys had collected, emerging from somewhere or other; they now surrounded me and gazed at me in stupefied silence. I looked back at them and then had again the strange feeling which I had experienced shortly before when studying the village at the foot of the cliff: they were Dogoni, that is, they belonged to a very special group of human beings; nevertheless, seen like that, in a circle in front of me, they appeared to be nothing more than ordinary African boys. In fact, since colour of skin and physical features, after one has been travelling in Africa for a little disappear and become 'invisible', they were just like boys anywhere in the world. At most one might have thought, from their swollen paunches with navels protruding like tumours in the middle of them, that they were poor and undernourished. And yet I knew for certain that that was not so.

These boys, so much like other boys, believed, for instance, that a single god, the god Amma, had created the world in the same way in which a potter creates his crocks. According to Dogoni cosmogony, indeed, the cosmos is merely crockery, beginning with the sun and moon which are two large basins, one of red copper and the other of white copper. Likewise these boys, who look so like boys of the same age in the rest of the world, really believe (as can be seen in Geneviève Calame Griaule's definitive study) this strange thing – and I say strange especially because it is believed in Africa – that the god Amma, the potter of the universe, fertilized Earth with speech. From this marriage, very difficult and indeed almost a failure, were born a pair of androgynous twins, the first of whom rebelled against his father to the point of forming an incestuous union with his own mother, Earth; while the second, on the contrary, supporting his divine father, remedied, by the sacrifice of his own life, the ills caused by his brother. Put to death and then resurrected, the 'positive' brother, as we may call him, created men, animals and plants. The 'negative' twin, on the other hand, was punished by being changed into a fox and condemned to lead a wretched, wandering existence.

These boys, in short, so innocent and natural-looking, believe (or at any rate form part of a society which believes) in a myth of the creation of the world which has many curious points of resemblance with the myths of Greece and the Eastern Mediterranean. Especially curious seems the idea that the creation of the world, at the very beginning, was a fiasco (original sin?); that two twins (Cain and Abel?) were at the source, one of evil and the other of good; that one of the twins was put to death and then resurrected and was the saviour of men by dying for them (Jesus?); and that the bad twin, subsequently transformed into a fox, rebelled against his own father and committed incest with his own mother (Oedipus?).

The moment has come at which we have to ask ourselves

why the Dogoni, having reached the point of formulating myths which were so 'humanistic', then came to a standstill at the myths themselves, whereas elsewhere there was a progression from myth to science, that is, from symbolical thought to truly scientific thought. By this we do not mean to suggest any superiority of the Europeans over the Dogoni, nor yet, as many people are tempted to do, the contrary. But merely to ask a question that is perhaps not altogether idle.

On consideration it seems to me that it is possible to indicate, as a reason for this, the substantial difference that exists between the cosmogony of the Dogoni and the analogous cosmogonies of our own antiquity. The Dogoni cosmogony is much more realistic, more naturalistic in fact, than any cosmogony of ours. The idea that the god Amma was a potter and that consequently the cosmos is crockery does not seem able to lead to a conception of the world as a system or order scientifically explicable, definable and measurable. Between the god Amma and Jove or Brahma or yet the God of Genesis, there is the same difference that exists between a craftsman who makes things with his hands, unpretentiously, according to empirical necessity, and the genius who brings into being from nothingness – or, if you prefer, from chaos – an autonomous world in accordance with a complex and deliberate creative will. Product of a careful observation of humble reality and not of a metaphysical consideration, the god Amma is too concrete and at the same time too bizarre to relate to anything but the modest human model that inspired him.

As further evidence, it should be observed how, with the Dogoni, speech is very much less abstract, very much more physical than the 'Word' in the Western sense. To the Dogoni, a thought, in the proper sense, does not exist. Thought consists of 'words that lie in the liver' or else of 'vapours'; and in fact the 'interior word' (that is, thought) would be made up of water, air, earth and fire. These four elements, in turn, would be fused in a voiced projection of personality, in other words, in sound. Moreover, analogously with the god Amma who is a potter, man who speaks is a weaver. Speaking, in fact, is synonymous with weaving in the anthropomorphic language of the Dogoni. The mouth is a loom; the teeth, the tongue, the palate, the throat are parts of the loom; the speech that emerges, after the loom, or the mouth, has done its work, is a woven tissue. It may be that, when we make use of the commonplace 'a tissue of lies', we are without knowing it speaking not in our own language but in Dogoni. Anyhow it is clear that a conception of speech that is so physiological and so physical can only lead with difficulty to rational, abstract thought.

But this dissimilarity, due to a different development of the myth, is more than compensated by the spontaneous and almost inexplicable sympathy shown by the Africans towards Europeans. Certainly there has been colonialism, with all its horrors; but it appears to be annulled, obliterated and forgiven by an invincible attraction. The willingness of communication on the part of the Africans seems all the more noteworthy when compared with the absolute recalcitrance of the American Indians and the ceremonious incommunicability of the East Asians. As we were walking back towards the place where we had left the cars, the boys were no longer content merely to follow us; but they gave us their hands and talked to us, partly as guides and partly as companions or, as they said, as *camarades*. They told us, without being asked, about their families, their farms, their domestic animals, their occupations. They asked us about ourselves with free and easy, correct curiosity, as between equals.

A small remuneration was, of course, expected at the end of our walk; but, as usual in Africa, the profit gained was not enough to explain the very natural, very trustful manner of approach. When I looked at the hand of my small companion enclosed in mine, and observed its pink palm, I could not help thinking, as on other occasions, that the African, like Plato's androgyne, was the irrational, primitive half of the rational, civilized European. And that the mutual attraction (Europeans, too, are attracted by the Africans, if one is to believe the so-called, well known 'Africa sickness') can be explained by this complementary situation.

24

Edward, Albert, Rudolph, Victoria

Mweya, January 1971

The region of the great African lakes, disposed in a semi-circle beginning with Lake Rudolph and then continuing with Lake Victoria, Lake Albert, Lake George and Lake Edward, is still today one of the wildest and most uninhabited in Africa. Even the names of these lakes, names of European princes and monarchs, confirm, by their too-recent character, this sense of historical emptiness and human desertedness, just as happens with the various 'lands' of the Arctic and the Antarctic which are also baptized with the proper names of kings and potentates of the period of so-called 'discoveries'.

Are they beautiful, these lakes? No, they are not. The sky of Africa, which is rarely serene and, when it is, is dimmed by the sultry heat, gives them a metallic colouring between grey and a leaden blue, oppressive and melancholy. Limitless, veritable fresh-water seas, it is impossible to see the end of them, so that the eye cannot take pleasure in the contour of their shores. In any case these shores are anything but picturesque. In general, too, it is almost impossible to reach them because they are marshy and thick with reed-beds. Besides, even where they are accessible there is nothing beautiful about them: they are steep, eroded banks of moderate height, tawny yellow and crowned with a tangle of bush. As always in Africa, the distinctive characteristic of these lake landscapes is sheer size. I have already mentioned the huge size of the lakes. In the same way the banks, the peninsulas, the islands, the promontories, the inlets, the bays are in long, straight lines, deserted, monotonous, endless. Yet, finally, by dint of repetition, sheer size becomes grandiosity.

These unbeautiful lakes have a fascination which is lacking in the smaller and far more picturesque European lakes. They give us a not too inaccurate idea of what we usually call prehistory. If it is true, as I believe it to be, that history is the name given by humanity to its own autonomy and victory over natural conditions, prehistory must be precisely the dependence of man on nature or actually his absence from it. But history is also time according to the measure of human life. Prehistory, consequently, is eternity. This word 'eternity', however, must not be given a solemn, terrifying meaning. Eternity in Africa is the absence of roads, of cultivation, of centres of habitation. It is the tree that has lived for no one knows how long and that suddenly collapses of its own accord in the bush and remains there rotting as it lies in the tall grass. It is the red, obscene cones of anthills scattered thickly in places where there might be gardens and fields. It is the marshes full of papyrus and reeds that make it impossible not merely to reach, but even to see the lakes except from distant heights. It is the tangled, evil bush country, the whitish plains, the wide prairies enlivened by the despairing gestures of dropsical baobabs. Finally it is the diseases, from bilharzia to the tsetse fly, from malaria to dysentery. Eternity, in fact, is squalid. The only exception to this squalor is the animals.

Hugging the shore, our launch came slowly out from the Kazinga channel, an arm of water connecting Lake Edward with the smaller Lake George. It was a cloudy day, the sky was overcast with dark, motionless cirrus clouds, the sun a livid halo. The waters of the lake were grey with gleams of brown, this being the colour of the weeds that appear on the surface. Starting from the mouth of the channel, Lake Edward begins to widen out and its shores grow steadily farther and farther from each other until the immense mirror of water invades the whole horizon. A sea, but without the pungent saltness, the powerful breath, the soul of the sea. We embarked at a little wharf of rotting beams, in the mud of a tiny harbour; then we proceeded at a very slow pace at a short distance from the lake shore. I noticed that the banks opened out here and there to form a grassy valley or a brief marshy beach. These valleys, these beaches seemed deserted. Yet, all of a sudden, with a leap of the heart, I saw in the distance, remote and dark against the pale background of the shore, an elephant. Yes, truly it was an elephant which, so to speak, was there all on its own, living its own natural life under our eyes, a wild elephant, ignorant of our presence, free.

Here I should like to point out that an elephant, when seen close to, is one thing, and an elephant in the distance is another. An elephant in, so to speak, the foreground, is an extravagant and apparently inoffensive animal for which one cannot help feeling affection. But an elephant glimpsed from far off immediately, by its mere presence, confers a prehistoric character upon the landscape. Before seeing the elephant, Lake Edward had been, for me, a kind of grey, melancholy sea, tiresome and oppressive. But as soon as I caught a glimpse of the small, dark, remote figure with its five legs (four legs and a trunk), Lake Edward at once became a landscape of the Quaternary period.

Meanwhile, our launch was slowly approaching the elephant which, nevertheless, although hearing and seeing us, did not alter its behaviour. It was grazing, and yet, owing to the extreme slowness of its movements, it might have been thought that it was meditating, contemplating, reflecting. Gradually it would stretch out its trunk, roll it round a clump of tall plants with leaves as straight and sharp as swords, effortlessly pull up the entire clump, roots and soil and all, roll back its trunk, insert the clump of plants and roots and soil into its strange mouth like the neck of an amphora, start chewing, its cheeks curiously flat and almost haggard, then after a moment reject the uneatable soil. Next it lifted one leg, slightly bent a knee and moved one step, again stretching out its trunk towards another clump. We approached still closer to it; I could have put out my arm and touched its trunk. An elephant, on close view, cannot but be both surprising and thought-provoking. What is the 'sense' of this animal? What is the meaning, for instance, of the contrast between the smallness of its organs of sight and the largeness of its organs of hearing? Between its microscopic eyes and its great, fringed, cartilaginous ears, like the enormous leaves of some aquatic plant? And why is its nose elongated to become a hand for solid objects and a pump for liquids? And what relationship exists between the strange usefulness of its trunk and the equally strange uselessness of its huge tusks? What significance has the evolution of this great beast (up to six tons in weight) in relation to the fact that it is exclusively herbivorous? Why are carnivorous animals small and herbivorous animals large? And, especially, why is it that the elephant does not 'look' savage, even if it is? – whereas the lion, the leopard and the hyena have always an obvious look of fierceness? Why, in short, does the elephant seem like a monument of timidity, of wisdom, of thought-fulness, of patience, when one knows that it can charge a motor-car and demolish it or, as recently happened in Uganda, crush under its feet a woman who had gone to fetch water from a river?

The elephant shook its ears; a little farther off, amongst the trees at the bottom of the valley, there emerged an enormous iron-grey back; a great head of the same colour appeared beyond it among the branches of a tree: the moment had come for us to depart, for herds of elephants, especially in places where they come to drink, are dangerous. But before we went away the elephant revealed one more thing to us: its own symbiosis with a little white bird with long, thin legs which hopped beside it and then, suddenly, with a brief flight, went and perched on its back. This brilliantly white bird lives not only on the elephant – that is, on what it can find in the mud trampled by the elephant, among the wrinkles of the elephant's skin and in the elephant's excrement – but also, in the same way, on the buffalo, the hippopotamus, the crocodile and the rhinoceros. There are various names for symbiosis: commensalism, mutualism, inquilinism, parasitism, according to whether symbiosis itself is based on the advantage to only one of the animals or both, or brings only an indirect advantage. What then would this little white bird be? A commensal? An inquiline? A parasite? To our eyes, anyhow, it appeared an extraordinarily attractive presence, with its fragility, its lightness, its immaculate whiteness beside the dark, muddy, enormous, powerful beasts with which it shares its existence.

Elephants in Uganda are not to be seen only on the shores of Lake Edward and Lake Albert. A few days later I drove by jeep through the forest of Maramagambo, in which the trees are neither big nor tall as in the equatorial forests but of the same proportions as the trees in our own woods. We drove along a narrow, muddy path on which gigantic footprints and enormous heaps of excrement revealed the disquieting presence of something disproportionate and monstrous in contrast to the 'temperate' character of the place. And then, all of a sudden, the jeep very nearly ran into the hindquarters of an elephant the foremost part of which had vanished completely amongst the leaves and branches. Farther on, the head of another elephant was suspended in mid-air, in a framework of foliage all speckled with sunlight and shadows. Farther on still, a grey, wrinkled flank made a background for the thin, snake-like lianas. We had plunged into the middle of a herd and we had not noticed it; nor – which was even more remarkable – had the herd noticed it.

Finally I saw elephants in the open, in the Kidepo plain on the borders of the Sudan. The landscape was more than ever the landscape of prehistory, of the Quaternary period: a boundless prairie and, on the horizon, bizarre mountains in the shape of extinct, black craters, of ruined castles, of rocks piled up one upon another. Again we were in a jeep. The grass on the plain was almost white, hoary, pallid, from which there emerged, here and there, the flat, thinly scattered umbrellas of thorny acacias. And then, suddenly, the elephants. There must have been twenty or thirty of them, a large herd. There were little ones, attractive as the young of any animal are, even though they were already enormous. There were females, feminine in their own elephantine way. And then the males, distinguishable by the length of their tusks that curve outwards on either side of their trunks that curve inwards. They were grazing, some of them on the ground and some among the branches of the trees. Then one of the elephants trumpeted: it was a deafening, strident, deep sound, a sound called forth by the passage of air through the colossal mucous membranes of its throat and trunk. At once three or four of the huge beasts then stopped grazing, drew themselves up in a line facing us, shook their ears and their trunks in a threatening way and – above all – *looked* at us. Yes, they looked at us, although their eyes can scarcely be seen, so small are they. But a small eye can be more threatening than a large eye. We took ourselves off.

25

The Didactic Nile

Kampala, February 1971

Africans shrug their shoulders when people speak of the so-called 'discoveries' of Africa. There was nothing to discover, they say; Africa has always existed, like Asia, with its civilization and its cultures; 'discovery' is an unsuitable word which goes to indicate, especially, a Eurocentric presumption. Perfectly true. But the fact remains that this word has been used for Black Africa; whereas, on the contrary, nobody would have dreamt of applying it to India or China. And why? Probably because the moment for the African cultures had not yet arrived; anthropological studies were still only beginning; Negro art had not yet influenced European artists. Anyhow, let us put forward two interpretations of the word 'discovery': one aggressive and the other receptive. The explorers of the nineteenth century, such as Stanley, Livingstone, Baker, Speke and Burton, 'discovered' the sources of the Nile in an aggressive sense. Nothing in their writings suggests that their explorations in Africa enriched them culturally, aesthetically, morally, etc. In reality they were there not so much to admire and understand as to annex and to conquer. Annexation and conquest were at first, so to speak, psychological; then political, military and administrative. But I myself, who am now travelling by car towards the sources of the Nile, will discover them, on the contrary, in a receptive sense. That is to say, I shall admire and understand. Receptive discovery, in short, is above all an experience that enlarges our horizons.

At last, the Nile. As the car reached the top of a hill, all of a sudden the famous river appeared, not very wide but already with the placid, majestic air which is one of its most noted characteristics. With its unmistakable colour – Nile green, in fact – its deep and as it were 'muscular' waters owing to the whirlpools and currents on its surface, it formed a wide, harmonious loop between banks of moderate height and decidedly pleasant-looking. But it must not be thought that this was the delightful, civilized pleasantness of the banks of the Arno or the Seine. African pleasantness has always something disquieting and savage about it. For example, the enchanting little beaches at intervals along the banks of the Nile undoubtedly look pleasant because of the picturesque arrangement of the great leafy trees that overshadow them and the romantic manner in which the green hills encircle them. But it would not occur to anyone to go and lie in the sun on these pleasant beaches, because the least that might happen to him would be to be seized and bitten by a crocodile, or butted by the horns of a buffalo, or trampled underfoot by an elephant, or cut in two, with a single bite, by a hippopotamus. Pleasantness, yes, but at a distance. The distance, in fact, that the launch carrying us towards the Murchison Falls maintained every time we came near these beaches.

We saw a triangular valley, half sandy and half grassy, with papyrus and reeds on its banks and trees away beyond at its deepest point, where it penetrated like a wedge between the yellow, eroded hills. Just as in a coloured plate in a book on zoology, there were animals side by side, each one on its own and ignoring each other, and displaying their most characteristic attitudes: an elephant with its trunk raised to snatch leaves from a tree; a buffalo lying in the mud; a hippopotamus in the act of rising out of the water on to the bank; a crocodile stretched out on a tongue of sand, motionless, its saw-toothed mouth wide open. Amongst the papyrus, in the meantime, appeared some birds with long, thin legs and big beaks. These Nile beaches are 'didactic'. All that is needed is the Latin inscriptions, in italics. For the elephant: *loxodonta africana*; for the buffalo: *bubalus syncerus*; for the hippopotamus: *hippopo-*

tamus amphibius; for the crocodile: *crocodilus niloticus*. The Nile, as a river, is too 'historical', too 'cultivated' for it to be possible, nowadays, for us to be able to get an impression of it at first hand, so to speak. It cannot be denied that cultural obstacles intrude between ourselves and this famous river. For example, as it is recorded in the Palestrina mosaic which, although it represents the Egyptian Nile, seems a perfect description of this Uganda Nile too, with its islands, its papyrus, its rocks, its waves, its wild beasts and everything else, in a one-dimensional perspective – in fact rather like that of the plates in the zoology books.

The two animals to be seen most frequently on the banks of the Nile are, obviously, the amphibious crocodiles and hippopotami. These latter have undoubtedly something comic about them. Their enormous great bodies are comic (two or three tons in weight), consisting absurdly of a colossal cylinder covered with bare brown hide and swollen to bursting-point, of four little crooked legs like a dachshund, and an excessively large head with shoe-shaped jaws. But their habits, too, have a touch of the ridiculous. They graze only at night; and it is amusing to watch a family of hippopotami moving away in the dark, heads lowered amongst the tall grasses of the Nile bank, then browsing in a space previously defined by a jet of urine; and woe to the outsider who risks crossing the boundaries of this species of olfactory enclosure.

By day, on the other hand, this idea of private territory combined with pasturage is given up, and the hippopotami, promiscuous as sheep, lie soaking in the water in herds of twenty or thirty, visible in small archipelagos of periscope-like eyes, horse-like ears and bare brown backs. A little African story is a very good illustration of the hippopotamus mentality. God did not wish the great beast to be amphibious because he was afraid he would devour the fish. So the hippopotamus promised God that he would be strictly herbivorous, and in proof of this, every time he defecated he would demonstrate to God that he had not eaten any fish. And this explains why, every time he defecates, the hippopotamus is careful to scatter his excrement, with his short tail, all round himself, and, naturally, on his companions lying in the water beside him. Thus God could see that he had eaten nothing but grass and had left the fish alone.

The hippopotamus' love-making, also, is comic. Two bulls or two he-goats butting one another with their horns are comprehensible and logical. But there is something ridiculous about hippopotami who are rivals in love when they push against one another with their huge wide-open jaws. They remain like that for hours, their mouths clamped together, with a thrust of two tons on either side; finally one of the two is victorious and the defeated one runs away. But sometimes he is pursued and bitten to death. A dead hippopotamus does not remain intact for very long. Men come from the neighbouring village and dig into the big carcase and carry away all the flesh from the skeleton. And so, in the end, there is left in the mud of the river a skeleton which, with its great ribs, resembles the wreck of a boat.

Crocodiles, on the other hand, are truly terrifying. It is no use telling oneself that they are merely enlargements of our own charming, inoffensive lizards. In reality size does not explain anything. The hippopotamus, for instance, is an enlargement of the ordinary pig, but it is not terrifying. The crocodile, on the contrary, is frightening. As much as seven or eight metres long, it lies on the beaches of the Nile, motionless as a tree-trunk. Its tail has a menacing look: one thinks of a blow from that tail. Its snout is equally menacing, with the teeth jutting out from the gums and the strange broken, curling line of its very long mouth.

We approached the crocodile. It remained motionless. Only its eyes showed that it was alive: its eyelids opened half-way, and its glassy, pitiless eye looked at us. Then, slowly, its mouth opened, went on opening and finally remained so, wide open, motionless. It is the only animal, as far as I know, that is capable of remaining with its mouth wide open for hours and hours. The rays of the sun crept into that mouth. birds perched on the teeth and poked about with their beaks in search of putrefied morsels. The crocodile stayed still, for it was a female and was hatching out its eggs. Even the idea of the egg is rather terrifying. From a hen's egg a pretty little chicken jumps out; but from a crocodile's egg there jumps forth a reptile that is already prepared to bite. We know that this is not the scientific point of view; and that even the crocodile, like any other animal, when looked at with an objective eye, so to speak, has its own beauty. But there it is. The crocodile is not lovable, at any rate by man.

Meanwhile, as our launch headed back upstream, there occurred more and more frequently, on the green surface of the water, strange bubbles of whitish-yellow foam. For some reason I do not know, they struck me as a phenomenon both inexplicable and disquieting, whereas a moment's reflection would have sufficed to clarify their origin. They grew thicker and thicker until the whole Nile appeared to be speckled with white, and suddenly I recalled the appearance of white 'objects' in the sea, during the journey to the Pole of Gordon Pym, the protagonist of Poe's novel. Finally we came to an island barring the river, and there we stopped. Beyond the island, the Nile was a seething mass of foaming, rapidly swerving waves. Farther on, behind the curtain of two or three wooded promontories, we saw the origin of the strange whitish bubbles: between two black rocks, an enormous, remote, silent explosion of shining foam, the Murchison Falls.

We turned back, disembarked, got into a car and went to see the Falls, upstream. We drove fast for a hundred kilometres through a dead forest: tree after tree after tree reduced to blackened spikes, to forks with broken teeth, to mutilated poles. The forest had been killed in order to kill the tsetse flies sheltering in its foliage. But the sleeping-sickness is still a danger, as is witnessed by the control points on the road, where two or three guards armed with butterfly nets searched our car for signs of the deadly fly.

From above and seen from behind, the Falls confirm the illusion of an explosion. Actually the Nile plunges from a great height into a fissure no wider than about twenty metres. But one has the impression that, on the contrary, it is being hurled upwards by an uninterrupted explosion. The clouds of white foam rise towards the sky, pierced by a perpetual rainbow. The thought occurs to one that the Nile, in rising to the sky, is in truth returning to its true sources. It is from the sky, in fact, that the Nile comes. It is true that it issues from Lake Victoria. But its waters, during the rainy season, fall from the sky.

26

The Mountains of the Moon

Entebbe, February 1971

The Mountains of the Moon provide a good example of the myths that can arise for the one and only reason of lack of communications. It has always happened in Africa: perhaps, in some particularly inaccessible region, it is still happening. In any place not reached by a track, in any place where people had to go on foot, a myth would be born. This juxtaposition of myth and going on foot may seem strange to some. My answer is that it is not so very strange because, almost always, 'going on foot' has meant 'not arriving'. The Mountains of the Moon were mythical because for centuries nobody had ever been there; and nobody had ever been there because, whether they came from the Red Sea or the Indian Ocean, or whether they started from Egypt, travellers, regularly, were lost on the way, killed by hostile tribes or by malaria, stopped by marshes or deserts, reduced by hunger and thirst or by the sun and the rain. Thus for centuries the Mountains of the Moon had remained unattainable and consequently legendary. It was said that they were extremely high, that the Nile gushed forth from them, that mines of gold and precious stones, reaching to the heavens, were to be found there, that there the world came to an end. Being unable to reach them physically, man reached them in imagination; on their peaks he planted the wondrous banner of fantasy.

And now there they were, the Mountains of the Moon. They ran right across the plain over which we were travelling by car on a smooth, convenient motorway. On the horizon, dimmed by sultry heat haze, rose a blue, pleasant-looking mountain range, of moderate height and strongly reminiscent of the Apennines in the neighbourhood of Bologna. And the legend? The legend is still with us. It expressed itself in our disappointment, in the usual question: 'Why, are those really the famous Mountains of the Moon?'

The motorway, unfortunately, did not last for long. The Mountains of the Moon, after being at one side of us, swung round behind us and disappeared. We turned off on to a crushed stone track and started driving through an entirely different landscape. We were among rounded hills that reminded us of poodles, for there were large shaven spaces and others covered with compact, swarming tea plantations. The track, of red crushed stone, went up and down all the time; one thought the hills must be coming to an end, instead of which, the more they went up and down, the more there were of them. Monotony, in any case, is the rule in Africa, that repetitive, bewildering continent in which everything is re-iterated until one's ordinary sense of reality reels and one is thrown into stupefied, visionary states of mind. That was what happened to me now. Seized with an irresistible desire to go to sleep, I looked at the track as it went up and down, at the tea plantations which clothed the swarming rotundities of the hills to the farthest horizon; and I said to myself that I should never arrive. Scarcely had this desperate thought formed in my mind than, ironically, reality took it upon itself to confirm it. On a steep slope, in the middle of the bush, the engine suddenly lost speed, the gears seized up, there was barely time to get the car to the edge of the ditch and then it stopped. I had been dreaming that I should not arrive. And then came the breakdown to tell me that my dream might well become reality.

And so it was, for it is one thing to have a breakdown on a road in Europe, among thousands of other cars, in industrial areas; and quite another thing in the solitudes of Africa, where, at most, there is a prevailing obligation, if you see a stationary car, to stop and ask if there is anything wrong. In Africa, a breakdown means a mechanic from a hundred or two hundred miles away, it means the difficulty if not the impossibility of reaching the mechanic, it means long waits of hours and hours on wild tracks used only by the mail vans, and then very rarely.

And this was precisely what had now happened to us. By now it was dusk, with a pale green sky against which the bizarre tangle of the bush stood out, black as Indian ink. The driver got out, opened the bonnet, looked, examined, shook his head. I, too, got out and asked him whether the damage was serious. He replied that he himself could not repair it, a mechanic was needed.

'And the mechanic – where is he?'

'At H . . . a.'

'How far is it to H . . . a?'

'Forty miles.'

'That's not much. We'll wait, and, the first car that passes, I'll get them to give me a lift to H . . . a and go and fetch the mechanic.'

He did not answer; with a look of discouragement, he went and sat down on the edge of the ditch. We all got out and started to wait. Half an hour went by, then an hour, and there was no sign of a rescuing car. Meanwhile night had fallen, the first stars were shining in the heavens; and then, as though summoned by a sixth sense – a 'social' sense, so to speak – and coming from goodness knows where, a number of peasants suddenly appeared from out of the bush. They were in their working clothes – that is, in rags – and they surrounded the car, examined it, listened to the driver's story, which he repeated to each newcomer. They looked at everything, they listened to everything, but, in the end, to my surprise, they did not go away. Nor did they stand there chattering, as generally happens in country villages, just to see how things were going to end. No, they gathered in a circle at a short distance from the car, they lit a fire and sat down round it. The driver sat down with them, but not without first introducing them to me one by one, with the perhaps not indispensable but significant explanation that these were good people, friends, kindly people who wanted to help him in a moment of difficulty.

I shook a number of hands, hands hardened and calloused from daily work with a pick, and received a number of dazzling smiles. Actually all these people had seized the opportunity of keeping company with the discouraged driver in order to have a little rustic sociable pleasure. They had been working all day; the usual hut, the usual wife and the usual children asleep in the dark awaited them – but here was something new. But when I said to the driver that no doubt a car would arrive soon and then I would go and fetch the mechanic, I received this despairing reply: 'At this time of day the mechanic won't want to come. He'll come tomorrow morning. And I myself will have to stay here and sleep in the car with the risk of being killed by bandits.'

'But what bandits?'

'The bandits who will come and carry off the engine, the wheels, the accessories.'

'Then come with us to H . . . a as soon as a car passes. Leave this car on the road.'

'I can't do that. I'm responsible for the car. I must stay here.'

And so this man, who looked so mild and calm, was being torn by an interior conflict: whether to stay and guard the car, doing his duty but at the risk of his life; or whether to go away and not do his duty. Doing his duty would, of course, mean keeping his job as a driver; by not doing it, he would lose his job. Sitting down in the circle round the fire, he added: 'Luckily these good people are here, for the moment.'

Someone who understands these things has told me that the typical outline of a conversation between African peasants is as follows. They meet and at once ask questions about the most important things: family, health, crops, etc. These reciprocal questions are reciprocally answered with extreme brevity because the important things are 'put aside' until later. Until when? Until later, when the moment comes. Having 'put aside' the important things, they can then carry on an animated conversation about this and that, or, as they say, 'have a chat'. It ends up, however, by the two people parting without having spoken of the 'important things'. When will they speak of them? They have been 'put aside' without the moment when they will be spoken of being specified. Possibly, then, at a subsequent meeting, or, indeed, never.

This was what was happening, so it seemed, round the fire at the edge of the road, in the chattering group of 'good people' who were keeping the driver company. The fire flared up and crackled, and the faces bending forward round the fire expressed great animation. Meanwhile the car that was supposed to be going to help us did not come. It is true that one mail van, crammed with people, went past; but it was going in the opposite direction. A dandy on a motor-scooter also went past. He looked like a gnome, so small was he, with a triangular, bespectacled face; he was wearing a blue shirt, lobster-pink trousers, green sandals, and his motor-scooter was painted yellow. We asked him to go and find the mechanic. He did not refuse, answered evasively, talked, argued, hesitated and finally went away. For him, too, the breakdown of our car had been a social occasion.

Then suddenly the situation cleared. An enormous champagne-coloured car flashed past beside me, stopped abruptly with a screech of brakes, a door opened and a gold cross gleamed on a black garment with a violet collar. A hand was outstretched, with a large amethyst on one finger. Learning that we were Italian, the bishop – for a bishop indeed it was – hastened to tell us, in Italian, that he would take us to H . . . a; so we must get in, we would find the mechanic, we would eat and sleep that night at his residence.

So we started off again at an immense speed, as if we were not in a car but on a flying carpet or some other magic vehicle. The bishop was extremely thin, with a face that looked as though it were made of various loose pieces of turned and polished ebony; these pieces shifted now for a smile, now for a glance, now for a grimace. He waved his hands, talked, asked questions. He wanted to know if I was a tourist and I answered that I was a journalist. Oddly, he then asked if I was a sporting journalist. On my replying in the negative, he fell silent.

At H . . . a, we found the mechanic in the usual 'main street' flanked by huts and bungalows with the shops of the Indians. The mechanic – he also was an Indian – took me aboard a ramshackle Japanese car, and in this way I travelled back over the forty miles to our own car. As I arrived, the whole of the gossiping circle seated round the fire rose and surrounded us. But foremost among them all came an individual who looked like a shepherd, very thin, solemn, armed with a crook and wearing a kind of sackcloth cloak. He spoke to me from very close, mouth to mouth; not knowing what to do, I shook his hand, then fumbled in my pocket to find the money he seemed to be asking for. But I was stopped by a chorus of protests; the individual was pushed away amid laughter and remarks of good-natured scorn and, as he went off grumbling, it was explained to me that he did not 'belong' there; that he did not form part of the group of 'good people' who had helped the driver; that he was a well-known profiteer and shirker, never present when required, always present when superfluous. In the meantime the damage, somehow or other, had been repaired. All the 'good people' held out their hands with great cordiality and we set off again.

For the third time I travelled those forty miles, arriving tired and hungry at the bishop's residence, a prefabricated structure on the outskirts of the town. I went into the refectory, much like any ordinary dining-room, perhaps, in a modest hotel, but with an added anaemic, ecclesiastical bareness, indefinable even though precise. There was a very long, narrow table, covered with floral-patterned oilcloth. The walls were blank save for one or two asymmetrical, casual Holy pictures. Television, radio, a refrigerator. A crucifix. The bishop had already eaten with my companions. And then, as I devoured some now cold spaghetti, facing the bishop who, cheerful and nervous, was laughing and talking and beating time with his fingers on the table, then I discovered the reason for that strange question of a little earlier, as to whether I was a sporting journalist. The bishop had been in Rome and was a football fan. He knew the names of all our most famous footballers. He asked and obtained information about the different teams from my companions, better acquainted with the subject of football than I was. Well, all that can be said is that, like religion, sport is an admirable means of opening communication between men of completely different countries and completely different cultures.

27

Which Tribe Do You Belong To?

Mbale, March 1971

'*Pour l'enfant amoureux de cartes et d'estampes*': this first line of Baudelaire's *Le Voyage* well expresses the fascination exercised by maps and, in maps, certain indications or even the absence of indications. One wonders, for instance, what the boys of the Middle Ages imagined when they looked at maps in which big blank spaces bore the legend: '*Hic sunt leones!*' I myself, during my journey in Uganda, felt the effect of this fascination in the strip of territory that runs right along the border with Kenya. This is the region that goes by the name of Karamoja. The red line of the road, or rather of the track, goes up and up on the map across a blank space entirely devoid of any names of centres of habitation, until it reaches Kidepo, near the border with the Sudan. Kidepo is a recently opened national park, with a 'lodge' where you can sleep but not eat. After some discussion, the fascination of the empty space prevailed and we decided to go to Kidepo.

My enthusiasm for this trip in the Karamoja, as I immediately realized, was not shared by Johnny, our African driver, a quick-witted, experienced man but excessively prudent, who had accompanied us on other peregrinations. Johnny came from Kampala, the capital; and he was, from every point of view, an inhabitant of the modern Africa, the Africa of neo-capitalist towns that have grown up here and there during the last twenty years. We had a confirmation of his character as a city-dweller when we went to his house, just before starting out. He lived in a small prefabricated house, in a street composed entirely of similar little houses, below the embankment of the motor-way. His wife, a handsome young woman in clothes of bright colours, all puffs and bulges and panniers, typical, here, of the dress of prosperous working-class women on the way to become lower middle-class, came up to bring him his fibre suitcase for the journey. Johnny introduced her to us with a brief wave of the hand, then said good-bye to her without embracing her; and we left. I looked at Johnny as he drove. He was very smart. He was wearing grass-green trousers and a yellow and blue checked shirt. The strong, crude colours had a fine effect in contrast to his skin which was the colour of roasted coffee. Johnny had a very expressive face; but it was not the 'sculptured' expressiveness of the African who lives in the bush; it was the 'psychological' expressiveness of the town-dweller. The former has to deal, above all, with nature; the latter with other men similar to himself.

From Kampala to Jinja we travelled by the motorway that leads to Nairobi; then we turned off on to the already mentioned track which, going up northwards parallel with the frontier of Kenya, reaches as far as the Sudan, the tea and cotton plantations came to an end, and the bush country began, tangled, commonplace, malignant. On the horizon appeared a strange mountain in shape like a turreted fortress, red and blue – possibly Mount Elgon which dominates the whole Mbale region. I said then to Johnny: 'You don't seem very enthusiastic about going into the Karamoja.'

He answered me with a slight smile, difficult to interpret: 'In the Karamoja there are people who are not too good.'

'Why not too good?'

'They're irritable and they have no liking for strangers. They carry spears. They think nothing of throwing a spear at you.'

'But they're Ugandans like you, aren't they?'

This time he did not reply. I knew what he would have replied if he had been conscious of certain social trans-formations in his country. It would have been like this: 'I belong to a certain tribe; the inhabitants of the Karamoja to another. It is true that we are all Ugandans and that Uganda is a nation with its frontiers, its capital, its government, its own flag. But, all the same, there is no good feeling between my tribe and the Karamoja tribe.' But instead of saying these true things, Johnny preferred to explain: 'You'll see at Kidepo. There is a whole regiment of our soldiers there, simply on account of those no-good people of the Karamoja.'

'But for what reason?'

'To prevent them crossing the Kenya border and making raids on the cattle of the Masai and the other Kenya herdsmen. They go into Kenya, they steal the cows, they kill the herdsmen and then go back to the Karamoja. Then the men from Kenya do the same to them. Our soldiers are there to stop this sort of thing.'

We were now driving along a track which at one moment cut straight across boundless plains covered with bush, and then curled round strange castles of rock all eroded and crumbling. There wasn't a house or a hut or a post to indicate any human presence. We were indeed in one of those regions which are marked on the map by a blank space without any names of centres of habitation. Nevertheless, in spite of the malignant, surly wildness of the place, the lions and other savage beasts, which once upon a time were implied by the legend '*Hic sunt leones*', failed to materialize. The only wild creature we happened to see was an ostrich, in a small clearing at the edge of the track. Extremely tall, its minute head taken up almost entirely by its large circular eye, its long neck bristling with scanty hairs, its bundle of a body supported, swaying, on the top of bare, sinewy legs like those of a champion walker, this strange creature, feathered but incapable of flying, stared at us for just one moment and then turned its rump towards us and ran off with its legs in the air (this is no exaggeration) to hide itself away in the bush.

We went forward, driving all the time at a high speed. The landscape became more and more strange, more and more lonely, more and more disquieting. If the moon had water and vegetation, it would have a landscape like this:

immense plains of a dark, gloomy green beneath vast skies in which hung very long cirrus-clouds tapering like cigars; horizons barred by ranges of conical mountains like extinct volcanoes. And then, finally, the 'not too good people' of whom Johnny had spoken.

Sometimes in small groups of two or three, sometimes alone, they appeared on the edge of the track from goodness knows where, the bush behind them and the bush in front of them. They were naked, completely naked except for a little piece of stuff that looked like sackcloth hanging over their chests and shoulders but open at both sides. Naked, coal-black, with no pubic hair, no hair in their armpits or on their chests; but with small pointed beards and, on the top of their heads, a sort of crest made of a number of little tresses of hair starting from the forehead and running in ridges across their skulls and reaching the backs of their necks. Naked; but armed with spears. They seemed to be shepherds; often they were surrounded by a few goats. But their nakedness must be understood. It is that of primitive peoples, not that of the Swedish or American nudists. This last is total, because it is civilized; *their* nudity, on the other hand, is archaic and, therefore, adorned, one might almost say clothed. It is a modified, embellished nudity, made significant and eloquent by tattooings, lacerations, necklaces, bracelets, ear-rings, rings, feathers stuck into the tresses on their skulls and chalky white smeared over half of their faces. Naked indeed they are, but their nakedness carried a very clear message of menacing, independent, distrustful pride.

And then the women arrived. There were three of them, preceded at a great distance by two men who were, as usual, armed with spears. We stopped. The men walked past beside us and disappeared along a path into the bush. The women lingered, seeming to wait until the men had vanished, then they stood still. They too had a small piece of material hanging over their chests and shoulders but leaving their bosoms and bellies bare; they kept one arm raised to support big gourds of water; their heads looked as though they had been decapitated and placed on a tray, owing to the backward-leaning position to which they were forced by the innumerable iron collars that towered up and from their chests to just below their chins. They were young, they had faces of great purity and simplicity, the expressiveness of which, unlike Johnny's, was not psychological but 'sculptured'. They looked at us with eyes that were half-closed and glistening with a look of malevolence; but perhaps this was an effect of the strange coagulated rheum which seemed to adhere to their eyelids. Then, all of a sudden, they smiled broadly at us, in a childish, innocent way, showing teeth of dazzling whiteness, and held out their hands. They had seen the camera of one of my companions, and they were asking for a reward for being photographed. Johnny, unconvinced, grumbled that we ought not to take photographs of them because the men do not wish it and might come back with their spears; but we paid no attention to him. The first photograph having been taken, the photographer was preparing to take another. There was an abrupt change of scene. The women held out their hands again for a second propitiatory shilling. On our refusal, they held up their fists and threatened us in an ugly fashion. Then they disappeared, arms raised to support the gourds thrown out, heads drawn back, hostile, hard, unpleasant. Johnny, triumphant, smiled contemptuously and, as he re-started the engine, commented: 'Bad people. Women, we know, need money. All the same, mustn't photograph them. It's dangerous.'

We drove for a further fifty miles through the bush and then came to the first Karamoja village in which, to Johnny's obvious distress, we stopped. The windows of the car remained closed; but gradually, from the crowded street, came the usual naked, spear-carrying individuals who leant forward to examine us. It was difficult to define the expression of their scrutiny. It was not exactly curiosity; perhaps, if anything, it was a kind of shrewd, surly inspection. Some of these faces were daubed with white; it is strange how the colour of the European skin, superimposed on the colour of the African skin, acquires a character of mysterious and rather sinister parody. Johnny, under this glowering, suspicious scrutiny, crouched in his seat like a smuggler under the eyes of the custom-house officers. He kept his hand on the gear-lever; it might have been thought that he was ready for a precipitate departure. One of the Karamojas put a question to him through the window. Johnny looked at him with a wooden expression and did not reply. I asked him why he did not reply. Distressed, he said: 'Can't understand them. I don't speak their language.' Finally, to his great relief, we started off again.

We arrived at Kidepo at sunset and went to the high ground on which the little building of the 'lodge' is situated. From this high ground one could see, on one side, a flat plain upon which – like the Christian encampments in the illustrations to the *Gerusalemme Liberata* – the tents of the Ugandan army were lined up in good order round a flagstaff; on the other side, the eye ranged over the immense plain of the national park, a dark, misty plain encircled by rocky, odd-shaped mountains.

Johnny, at Kidepo, now behaved exactly like a tourist on foreign ground. He went with us to the shop at the lodge and, while we bought our usual corned beef and bread for supper, he acquired a spear-head and had it wrapped up 'to take as a present for my wife'. Then we went to eat our food in the bar-room. Through the windows we could see, down below, at the edge of the park, a number of antelopes as big as oxen filing past in the red, steamy evening light. Inside the room only one small table was occupied. Three Africans dressed in the European manner were sitting round a tray upon which was an entire roast kid; they were tearing off pieces of it with their hands. Then one of them saw that I was cutting the corned beef with my hunting knife and asked me, in good English, for the loan of it. I rose and handed it to him. He took it, looked at me, and then, courteously and punctiliously, inquired: 'And you – which tribe do you belong to?'

28

The Stripes of the Zebra

Kampala, March 1971

We reached the Mission at night, after a drive across the great plain. Two Italian missionaries welcomed us in the dark, in a wide courtyard surrounded by the low, one-storey buildings of the Mission. Just at that moment the headlights of a lorry shone out behind the gate through which we had passed a moment before. The gate was thrown open again and the lorry came into the courtyard. 'Fresh meat,' said one of the missionaries. The lorry was driven by an African; another African was sitting beside him, holding a rifle between his knees. The lorry stopped, the back flap was lowered and there, by the light of a lantern, I could see that it was indeed a matter of fresh – or rather, as they say, 'chilled' – meat: inside the lorry, thrown one on top of another, stiffened in death, were two large antelopes and a zebra. One of the missionaries climbed up into the lorry, inserting his feet among the rigid limbs of the animals; the other was now manoeuvring a small van so as to get it close beside the poachers' lorry. I went closer. The poachers' lorry was black with congealed blood underneath the head of the zebra; the smell of blood, acrid, noxious and moist, like that of soaked linen in a hospital, made me draw back with a feeling of nausea. One of the poachers also climbed up into the lorry and helped the missionary move the zebra into the Mission van. The zebra was as big as a horse but more solid; it was only very slowly that it could be moved. For a short time I had the animal's head right under my eyes, and then I was struck by a curious fact. The black and white stripes (to tell the truth, they are a very dark brown) which give the zebra its beauty and which are so elegant and so precisely arranged, especially on the muzzle and on the legs, seemed now, with death, to be no longer 'arranged'. This was not true, of course; it was an effect of the havoc caused by the shot on the animal's head, lacerating the skin and sticking it together in patches, and producing a large blotch of congealed blood all round the big, half-closed, glassy eye. But the impression still persisted: that the stripes were out of place, rather like the check pattern of a badly cut sports jacket made by an inexpert tailor. I realized thus how fragile is nature's beauty. The black and white stripes of the zebra are like the wings of a butterfly, which need only the strong pressure of two fingers to destroy their colours.

Meanwhile the zebra, by hard pushing, had been transferred from the poachers' lorry to that of the Mission. As the exhausted missionary looked at his bloodstained hands, I asked him: 'Is it good, zebra meat?'

'It's like horseflesh. The antelope is better.'

'Why didn't you take the antelope?'

'The Mission is poor. The antelope is more expensive. We have to be content with the zebra.'

Later, sitting at table in the Mission refectory, we spoke of the Sudanese refugees, members of the tribes in revolt in the province of Equatoria, who for some years had been crossing the frontier and taking refuge in Uganda. They are Christian, animist Africans who are fighting for autonomy against the Musulman Arabs of the Sudan. the Sudanese army is, of course, stronger; but the African tribes who, it seems, are receiving help from the Israelis (on the principle, 'the enemies of my enemies are my friends'), give them food for thought with a cruel guerrilla warfare which in the past has come very near to genocide. Recently the Sudanese government has changed its policy and has let it be known that the civil war may be considered to be over. According to the missionaries, however, this is not so. 'Again a few days ago,' said one of the missionaries, 'about seven thousand people crossed into Uganda.'

'Where do they go?'

'Wherever they can. They disperse among the villages. Or they are received into the refugee camps.'

'How many of them are there in Uganda?'

'It's said that there are about two hundred thousand, but that is including the Watussi refugees, from Burundi.'

'Those of the superior minority who were done down by the inferior minority?'

'So it's said.'

'And is it possible to see these refugees?'

'It's not easy. The Uganda government accepts them; but it doesn't want to have trouble with the Sudanese government.'

I went to bed with the two pictures confused, for some reason, in my mind, that of the dead zebra and that of the Africans turned out of their villages. Next day, in the outskirts of Moroto, a large town to the north, by sheer coincidence we came upon a small encampment of Sudanese refugees.

They were of the same Nilotic stock as the inhabitants of the Karamoja. In the dust of one of those immense denuded spaces that surround African towns they had built a kind of little *bidonville*. The idea of the village had survived, but it was all confused and obliterated and shattered. The huts were not arranged in any recognizable order, but irregularly crowded together, in some places more thinly scattered but in some places more numerous. They were made of straw, but the straw was untidy and scanty and the roofs were of corrugated-iron held in place by large stones. The ground between the huts was not clean but scattered with rubbish; and the naked children were playing there with their faces and eyes full of dust. The women were attending to their usual domestic jobs with an air of unwillingness; many of them were huddled together in the shade of the mango-trees, gossiping and selling microscopic quantities of rotten fruit or seeds or red peppers. As for the men, they were squatting on their buttocks and the soles of their feet, like tired vultures, near the doors of the huts. They stared into the air as though following the improbable mirage of their missing herds. I went up to the women who were sitting under the mango. They had only a few of the rings, collars, garlands and other ornaments which they generally wear with such pride. They were dressed in rags. Here again there was the idea of African femininity, but gone astray, confused, shattered. Laughing, they held out their hands; they were sitting with their legs wide apart, legs and breasts pointing in different directions; they were assuredly more ill-mannered than innocent. Persistently the recollection of the dead zebra and its disordered stripes came back into my mind. This little African community, too, had been stricken to death, like the zebra. And everything that had previously fitted together, that had been connected and linked – huts, occupations, children, men, women – was now undone, disconnected, disarranged. The mysterious, magical orderliness of life had been replaced by the disorder of death.

That same day, after a long drive through the bush, this impression of mine was confirmed. We came out suddenly into a circular clearing in which there were no more than four huts. We stopped to look. The huts were round with conical roofs, all made of thick, well-plaited, new straw of a fine light colour. They were arranged symmetrically at the four corners of a perfect square within the circle of the clearing. The floor was of beaten earth, cocoa-coloured, smooth, compact, perfectly clean. In front of each hut was an iron tripod; beneath each tripod a fire was burning; suspended from each tripod a pot was boiling. Spades and other agricultural implements were leaning in order beside the doors of the huts; gourds for water were hanging from nails. In one corner of the clearing were posts fixed upright in the ground to support a grating of branches upon which recently washed pots and pans, dishes, glasses and cups were laid out to dry. At this point it should be said that cleanliness and order in Africa are more visible than in Europe because Africa is lacking in light and shade and the contours of objects are, so to speak, outlined in space by the light. Thus, in this group of huts, I was once again struck by the almost dazzling luminosity of Africa. All at once a woman came out from one of the huts. She was young, tall, robust, with a piece of blue material wound round her breast and hips. She had all the customary rings, collars, bracelets and ear-rings, as well as the crest of little locks of hair lining her skull from her forehead to the back of her neck. She smiled, greeted us, and then went to a corner of the clearing where a big tree-trunk lay on the ground. She took hold of an axe and, holding the tree-trunk firm with her bare foot, proceeded to split it and chop it in pieces. She raised her arm holding the axe and struck with precision at a very short distance from her own foot. Then she stopped, and with an attractive, vigorous twist of her bust turned, smiled at our driver and spoke to him. Suddenly a rustling of leaves made me look up. There were two or three monkeys leaping and chasing one another amongst the highest branches of a great tree at the edge of the clearing. For some reason I imagined then that this rustling sound was followed by rifle-shots and that soldiers then burst out from the bush, upset the tripods, threw the woman to the ground and raped her, set fire to the huts. Once again there came to mind the sight of the dead zebra and of its stripes that no longer coincided.

Soon afterwards we finally left the dark thicket of the bush and came out into the emptiness and light of the great plain. This was like an immense steppe, almost white, as though bleached. In the tall grass, scattered here and there but with a curious chance regularity, were big round bushes, dark green, which had grown up round the twisted trunks of the thorny acacias, in the transparent shade of their scanty umbrella-shaped foliage. And there, only a few metres from the track, was an entire herd of zebra. Some of them were curled up on the ground looking as though they were resting; others were standing upright, grouped as horses group themselves, some head to tail and some tail to head. We stopped to look at them. How beautiful were their black and white stripes, with what beauty and refinement did they fit together! Then, at the sound of our engine, they all ran off, both those that were lying on the ground and those that were standing up. They fled, carrying off with them, at a gallop through the tall grass, their black and white stripes. But, even as they fled, their stripes still fitted together, they remained linked. Terror, the instinct of self-preservation, were still a part of life.

29

Encounters at Malindi

Malindi, April 1971

It was early in the morning. The sky was still vaguely misty; the sea was green as a meadow, its long waves fringed with white foam which, starting from remote coral banks, rolled lazily in, like murmuring carpets of water, to spread, exhausted, on the shore. The sun rose behind the green colonnades of date-palms; the immense beach caught the light and every fold of sand cast a faint pink shadow. In this early morning hour, from the french windows of the hotel – which was in sham Arab style, built in semi-circular form on the dunes – there came out, a few at a time, some fair-haired children, three or four very thin old men, and a couple of gouty matrons. Each of them was carrying a book. They went quickly to the groups of deck-chairs set out under big umbrellas all round the swimming-pool, threw the books on to the chairs and walked quietly back into the hotel. The 'Scramble for Africa', in fact, continues, even if with different ends and means. Once it was a rush for the occupation of territories; today, more modestly, a grabbing of deck-chairs.

And so, when I arrived later with the intention of lying in the sun, I found all the places already taken though still deserted. I took the opportunity of seeing what the British middle class reads during a holiday in an ex-colony. There is a very expressive word in American slang which describes this kind of reading: crap. The books which the guests in my hotel made use of to seize a place in the sun were all 'crap', in other words, best-selling sentimental novels, cloak-and-dagger tales, thrillers, biographical romances. I was struck by the complete absence of books on Africa and the Africans. And yet, if one travels and stays in Africa, one acquires what is (to me, at any rate) an irresistible curiosity to know more about the so-called mysterious continent. Yet it is precisely the English scholars who have written the best books on the subject, as can be seen in the splendid bookshops in Mombasa, Kampala and Nairobi. So there it is: the middle-class people staying in the hotel wish to ignore the fact that Malindi is some thousands of kilometres from Brighton. A jest, of what we may term 'unconscious' colonialism.

Since there was no room under the big umbrellas, I decided to take a walk along the seashore. I went down from the sand-dunes, across the beach. The curve of the coast was hidden, at its two ends, in a golden mist of sand and light. On one side the beach, white and deserted, continues between the sea and the dunes, as far as a hazy promontory; on the other, equally white and deserted, it runs along beside the semi-circle of bizarre hotel buildings in Arab, Polynesian or Spanish style, to the distant outline of the houses, domes and minarets of the old town. I took off my sandals and for fun followed the ebbing of a wave which, shortly before, had spread half-way up the beach. I found myself in the middle of an enormous expanse of glittering sand, while the water beyond me continued to retreat with a gurgling backwash. I do not know whether it was the effect of the sun or of metallic particles; but certainly the wet sand had a colour like that of dark, coppery gold, the whole surface being finely chequered with oblique squares made up of millions of minute lozenge-shapes. Hopping here and there upon this golden mirror were fussy, intent sea-birds of immaculate whiteness, with long, thin legs and long beaks. Now and then I saw in the sand a round hole and, beside it, a small heap of disturbed sand. Then the maker of the hole crept out cautiously: a big crab of a pale pink shaded with brown. Walking backwards, it proceeded to follow the still retreating wave. I kicked it back again. Then, courageously, it faced me, lifting its big claws into the air. A surge of water took pity on it, turned it over and swept it away in its liquid bosom, amongst the black débris and the green seaweed. I resumed my walk.

Encounters began. First came a girl in a topless costume. Neither beautiful nor ugly, possibly not very young, dark, with a pale, plump body unevenly reddened by the sun of the tropics, she exhibited her bare bosom as she walked beside a bearded young man with whom, it seemed, she was engaged in a very serious discussion. Part of her hair fell over her shoulder, part over her chest. Every now and then she shook her head, and then one of the two locks of hair took the place of the other, covering the uncovered part of her chest and uncovering the covered part of her back.

As I went on I met dogs with their masters. The dogs were all thoroughbreds, most of them young and handsome; their masters, who had probably lived at Malindi for many years, were all elderly. There were old ladies and younger ones, old soldiers living on pensions, old retired officials. Then two magnificent basset hounds, brown with white spots, comic-looking with their big crooked legs and their long bodies with bellies skimming the sand. Then an improbable pair, a gigantic grey and pink mastiff and a microscopic black chihuahua like a minute, lively little imp. An Afghan, at the same time both slender and woolly. A large family of poodles, white, black and brown. There was always a moment when all the dogs met, forming as it were a little canine parliament in the middle of the beach. They sniffed each other, examining each other and wagging their tails in a friendly, sociable way. Meanwhile their masters, misanthropically, avoided greeting or talking to one another; they continued on their melancholy walks, the dog-leads under their arms.

After the 'topless' girl, after the dogs, it was the turn of a young African of fine appearance on the watch for an adventure. There were always two or three figures in a sort of échelon formation, along the beach, idly waiting, looking around. The one that morning was in black trousers and a white shirt; he held a stick in his hand and was drawing ornamental flourishes in the sand. All of a sudden a middle-aged woman appeared, a European, wearing a green bodice and very wide, bell-shaped yellow trousers. The brim of her big straw hat swung up and down at every step over her downcast eyes, as she advanced laboriously over the dry portion of the beach. As soon as the young African who was writing in the sand with his stick saw the woman, he moved quickly, in a diagonal direction. The woman did not seem to be aware of him; but she visibly slackened her pace so as to contrive that her path, by forming a perfect acute angle with that of the African, allowed the latter to join her. Which, in due course, happened. The African took his place at the woman's side and spoke to her. She did not turn, she did not lift her face under the brim of the hat, she did not stop, but she did answer him: I could see this from the movement of her lips. And thus, side by side, talking, they went off; he turned towards her as she walked with head bent, without looking at him.

They went off with a deliberate slowness that was more significant than any sort of impatient speediness, as they walked along the shore. I gazed at them spellbound; I watched them go farther and farther away; finally, in the misty cloud of sand and light and foam from the sea, all I could distinguish was the flapping of the woman's yellow trousers. Then, far away, where the hotels came to an end and the continuation of the shore was deserted, they turned aside across the beach, still with the same slowness, and vanished amongst the dunes.

Another encounter: a girl on horseback accompanied by her father. She was fair-haired and small, thick-set and robust; she was riding a big black mare; she was wearing a sleeveless pullover, shorts and boots of undressed leather with her bare knees gripping the saddle. Her hair, blonde and compact, bounced up and down on her shoulders. Her father followed her on a white horse dappled with grey. He was a corpulent male replica of his daughter: the same hard brow, the same little snub nose, the same square chin. They galloped high up on the beach where the sand was deeper. They too made their way towards the more deserted part of the shore. They too, when they reached the point where sea, sky and sand became blurred in the wind and the light, vanished among the dunes.

And finally the Indian women, having a bathe together with their children. They crossed the beach in their saris, of white, lilac, pale green or pale blue. Bundled up in this way, and with their enormous black eyes, they looked like big caterpillars. They entered the water without undressing, and their wet saris immediately became transparent, revealing other, more intimate swathings, of white cotton. In the sea they dispersed into groups of two or three, holding the children by the hand. A boisterous little wave came rolling in; the Indian women struggled clumsily, fell down, went under, rose up again, groping and shouting. They were like nuns ill-accustomed to the sea, the sun and nature, bathing in a group, well away from indiscreet eyes.

The sun had put the last clouds to flight, and it was scorching. I went up again across the beach and, by a path between two hotels, reached the road that led to Mombasa. Here it was all in shade; and I started walking along beside the prefabricated bungalows, new and clean, of the little English Malindi which had grown up at a few kilometres' distance from the old Arab Malindi. It was the hour at which the European women go by car, accompanied by their children, to do their morning shopping. They stop in front of the bright shops with big windows, so different from the dark bazaars of the Arab town, leave the children in the car, make their purchases of tinned stuff, of food wrapped in cellophane, of bottles, in the supermarket, throw the packages on to the back seats, leave again in a hurry. They stop at the bank for money, at the post office for the post, at the hairdresser's to make an appointment. They turn their big cars of the 'station-waggon' type, and then, by country lanes, take their way to their family cottages buried deep in small gardens overflowing with tropical flowers.

The African women, on the other hand, go on foot, they too to do their morning shopping, making their way towards the noisy, disorderly little market in the Arab town. They walk in single file, empty baskets on their heads, their hips swathed in bright-coloured stuffs, their busts bare. One of their breasts, the one with which they suckle their baby, is longer than the other by a good hand's breadth. Their faces are black as coal, masculine, distressed-looking, as of men who have toiled and suffered much. The baby in a shawl on their back sticks its head out and, turning its eyes this way and that, gazes quietly and attentively at the spectacle of the world.

I stopped at a barrow, bought a mango and ate it as I walked. I nibbled at the yellow, slightly acid pulp and threw away the enormous stone, like an oval pebble from a river bed. And this gesture reminded me of another journey in Africa. We had crossed the trail followed by the slave caravans a hundred years ago. The trail, here and there, was shaded by magnificent mango-trees with rich, dark, motionless foliage. That day someone told me that these mango-trees had sprung from the stones of the fruit which the slaves, in their chain-laden procession, had eaten during their march to the coast.

30

Lift the Weight off Your Heart

Dar-es-Salaam, April 1971

The big hotels of mass tourism that have been built here
and there in Africa during the last years are like the
façades which Prince Potemkin is said to have erected for
the worthy reception – or rather, the deception – of Catherine
the Great. Behind Potemkin's façades were the frozen pools
and the huts of Petersburg. Behind the tourist hotels of
Africa lies the emptiness of the great plains, with its
wretched villages, its lurking diseases, its terrifying super-
stitions. I thought of these things as I wandered round the
hall of the main hotel in Dar-es-Salaam, one of the largest
in Africa. Why, indeed, so much grandeur, so much luxury?
I said to myself that, in contrast to the missionary who
shares the African's life and suffers with him, in contrast to
the surviving rich man on safari who wants to kill his wild
beasts and nothing more, the mass tourist is psychologically
'fragile': to protect himself from a sense of guilt he has
neither the charity of the former nor the cynicism of the
latter. Furthermore, why the sense of guilt?

Again, it is clear that the majority of people become
sensitive in relation to the power to which they aspire or
which they already hold. For this reason they do not like
to find amusement in the midst of sufferings and privations
for which, precisely because they have power, they might
feel themselves to be in some way responsible.

Anyhow, even if it is without the slightest sense of guilt,
we too were mass tourists. So we did something that mass
tourists do. We decided to spend the day on an Indian
Ocean beach. We would go to Zanzibar, with its perfumed

air, its white coralline beaches, its green sea and its forests of palms. But the departure times of the aeroplanes did not suit us. We made shift, therefore, with Bagamoyo, about a hundred kilometres from Dar-es-Salaam.

Bagamoyo, it seems, means 'Lift the weight off your heart'. At first sight, something like 'See Naples and die'. But Africa is not a gentle continent. The meaning of the name 'Bagamoyo' acquires a sinisterly sardonic sense as soon as one remembers that, a century ago, it was to this place that the slave caravans were conducted. And that, also at Bagamoyo, the slaves were put on board the small, swift Arab ships to be taken to Zanzibar and there sold by auction. Nothing, then, of the 'See Naples and die'; if anything, the no less sinisterly sardonic *'Arbeit macht frei'* ('Work makes you free') which was written over the entrance to the Nazi extermination camp at Auschwitz. But this 'weight' that was lifted from the heart when you arrived at Bagamoyo – was it really, then, merely an irony? To a great extent, yes; but one cannot exclude the possibility that, to the unfortunate arrivals at Bagamoyo after the immensely long, murderous march across the continent, even slavery, now certain and inevitable, might appear as a kind of horrible relief.

We left in the morning. The road map promised an asphalt road as far as Bagamoyo; we were sure of arriving there in little more than an hour. An illusion! About twenty kilometres from Dar-es-Salaam the asphalt came to an end and the track began. Let us be clear, however, about this track. The tracks of the high plateau, smooth and hard, of very fine crushed stone, are almost better than the motorways. But the track to Bagamoyo was of sand, a dry, very fine sand like that of the seashore, in which the mail vans had dug two deep furrows with their massive wheels, and it was necessary to stay in these furrows, otherwise there would be trouble. So we had to drive at twenty kilometres an hour, taking care not to let the car come out of the wheel-tracks that meandered about in the sand. The sea, rough and troubled, was close by, on the other side of a green strip of plantations – close by, but under a pale, restless sky disturbed, to all appearance, by the sea winds.

Luckily we were passing through a thickly inhabited area. Often, among the trees, there was a glimpse of a conical thatched roof, or the flat corrugated-iron of some hut sunk deep in the luxuriant tropical undergrowth. Or there would be a clearing surrounded by huts, with children and domestic animals frolicking on the beaten earth, among the fetid puddles. As always in the country, the people stay at the sides of the track, to see what goes on. There were groups of men crouching in the shade of the mango-trees, behind little piles of fruit for sale; and groups of women standing up, with babies in their arms. Unfortunately, however, there are not many things that can happen on a track in Tanzania. A country bus may go past – certainly an event not devoid of interest, especially if, as almost always occurs, the shaky, many-coloured vehicle is crammed full, with people exploding, so to speak, out of the windows. A large, funereal-looking car hired at Dar-es-Salaam by a family to take them to some tribal festivity in their native country may also pass through; and this too is an event not to be despised, especially if the women are dressed in the European style which has recently been deplored by student demonstrations in the capital. Finally it may happen that a government car may drive past, carrying some well-known official personage, enveloped in his own power like the car in its cloud of sand; and this certainly would be the most welcome occasion even if also the least likely, seeing that it might provide an opportunity for manifestations of democratic sympathy. But what can happen, on a track, comes to an end here. So, finally, the real happening which is always new is not so much the passing of this or that car; but what may happen to the car itself as it passes. To put it briefly, it may get choked up with sand.

In a case like this the car, driven by an inexpert hand, leaves the track and comes to a halt; while its wheels, urged uselessly on, go round and round vainly in the sand. This, as we have observed, is a real event and, without being actually sensational and upsetting, can cause a certain movement. The men who had been sitting in the shade of the mango run up: someone places palm-leaves under the wheels, someone else pushes. The women watch the men's efforts and comment upon them. Finally there is somebody who goes on talking about his own affairs with somebody else, though all the time close to the sand-choked car. A little like those characters in the pictures of the Primitives who converse quietly on one side while, in the foreground, a martyr, on his knees and with his hands tied behind his back, presents his neck to the executioner's sword.

Luckily we were not the victims of a misfortune of this kind, but we were the cause of one. At a bend in the track, suddenly we found ourselves face to face with a small car driven by a middle-aged European, alone. We stopped and he stopped. The wheel-tracks in the sand, deep and winding, were at that point only two, so that if one of us did not move to the side, a collision was inevitable. But avoiding a collision meant, obviously, leaving the track and plunging into the sand. After a moment without movement, our driver played a trick; he made a feint, as in a duel with swords. He pretended to be moving – but very slightly – to the right. His opponent fell into the trap; ingenuously he moved – but seriously – to the left. His car left the wheel-tracks and went and hit a tree. Immediately, from every direction, helpful, willing people who had been following our duel with hopeful anxiety, appeared on the scene. We left them busily occupied round the stranded car and resumed our journey.

We passed plantations of coconut-palms, scattered, stunted trees with thin trunks bearing, at their tops, a few pointed leaves and, underneath the leaves, bunches of big fruit. Then suddenly, at a bend in the track, we saw Bagamoyo. I had heard it spoken of, positively, as a small town. Instead of which, it is no more than a tiny village, with two short parallel streets flanked by the usual bunga-lows and shops, starting from the sheds of the market and coming to an end in the bush, a little farther on. In the Indian general store we bought corned beef and bread for our luncheon, and then started exploring. We discovered that the old Bagamoyo of the times of German colonialism was disintegrating and crumbling amongst tall plants and groups of palm-trees at a short distance from the village. There were old Arab villas, completely abandoned, their gardens smothered in weeds, their gates broken down and rusty, their window-panes shattered. Or again, there were administrative offices, decayed and neglected, built nearly a century ago by the Germans, chalky white and in a vaguely Oriental style, with battlements and pointed arches and arcades, their windows furnished with complicated wooden gratings which, since there was no air-conditioning, had to provide at the same time both shade and ventilation.

In one of the prose poems of *Une Saison en Enfer*, Rimbaud imagines that he is looking at '*le ciel bleu et le travail fleuri de la campagne*' through the eyes of a convict, '*avec son idée*'. That is, through the eyes of a man who has been punished, persecuted, outlawed. At Bagamoyo, as though to counteract the feeling of facile exaltation inspired by the beauty of the place, one cannot help looking at the beach, the palm-trees, the sky, the ocean 'through the eyes' of the slave, that is, the eyes of the man who knows that never again can he be free. We went down a path to the sea, and there, a few steps from the beach, came upon a gigantic tree with round, coarse, dark leaves and a trunk so thick that the branches, rising upwards, looked as if they were joined directly to the roots which, equally stout and powerful, plunged downwards into the ground. An iron ring was fixed into the trunk; to this ring the slaves' chain was secured, while, squatting beneath the tree, they waited to be put on board ship. We sat down on the sand at a short distance from the mango-tree and looked round. How beautiful it is, the Bagamoyo beach! A shining strip, it follows the curve of the bay, between the stormy sea and the slanting palms which are dimmed, as far as the eye can reach, by the misty cloud of sand and wind-blown foam. How beautiful and how deserted! For a moment I forgot to look at the landscape through the eyes of the slave; and I said to myself that anyone who has not seen dazzling sunlight sparkling on the leaves at the tops of palm-trees, at the moment when the wind turns them back, does not know what happiness is. But, immediately afterwards, the 'idea' of the slave came back to me. For him, the ancient and never-contradicted game of analogies and symbols could not work. The sea, emblem of freedom, at the very moment when he looked at it and said to himself that beyond those blue waves slavery awaited him for the whole of his life – the sea, at that moment, acquired the opposite significance. And those bunches of feathery leaves ruffled by the wind and lashed by the sun against the background of burning sky, did not, with their brilliance and their tumult, inspire him with a sense of happiness but of anguish, of anticipated homesickness.

31

The Slave Coast

Lomé, January 1972

In Africa, during the nineteenth century, one could still travel in the manner of Herodotus, not through well-defined nations but from one vague tribal area to another. When Herodotus gives, for instance, a list of names of the peoples of Libya – Adimarchidi, Giligami, Aziri, Asbisti, Cirenei, Auschisi, Bacali, Nasamoni, Psilli, Garamanti, Maci, Gindani, Lotophagi, Ausei, etc. – he speaks of a world without frontiers in which the peoples were continually mixing according to the various nomadic trends of peace and war. A hundred years ago this was still the situation in Black Africa. Empires and kingdoms, it is true, had not been lacking in the past; but they had concentrated round some powerful personality or family. When the former died, or the latter fell into decadence, they dissolved without succeeding in creating a historical exception within the rule of nature.

With colonialism, there were invented round the treaty tables about thirty nations, or rather colonies, completely mysterious to the ignorant inhabitants but perfectly clear to the powers which had partitioned them on a basis of their own exclusive interests. Nevertheless it is a noteworthy fact that, once they had obtained independence, not a single one of the ex-colonies rejected the colonialist frontiers and returned to the former tribal confusion.

Why was this? When all the ill has been spoken of colonialism that it deserves, it has to be recognized that, in the end, the Africans preferred the institutions and organizations imported from Europe to the tribal traditions towards which – perhaps precisely because they are still very strong – they entertain a curious, contradictory mistrust. For example, the civil war in Nigeria (an artificial nation created by Britain), which was an attempt to found a nation on a tribal basis, was, among other things, a symbolic contest, valid for the whole of Africa, between two different conceptions of nationality, the one previous to colonialism, the other subsequent to it. The defeat of Biafra was the defeat of the tribal conception.

Probably the nations will endure. Nevertheless, often, travelling in Africa, one cannot escape from a sense of unreality. Take, for instance, the five nations through whose territory I crossed when I travelled by car along the coast of the Gulf of Guinea, from the Ivory Coast to Nigeria. Of these five nations let us consider Togoland. This is a small French-speaking country, fifty thousand square kilometres in extent and with a million and a half inhabitants. Togoland has a coastline of only fifty kilometres, and stretches six hundred kilometres from south to north. A wedge-shaped country, Togoland, like the other coastal countries, is formed of strips, like a Venetian blind: first a strip of sea, then of sand, then of forest, finally of prairie; but it is also formed of patches, like Harlequin's cloak, as regards its population. A modern Herodotus might, like the ancient one, find amusement in enumerating the peoples of Togoland: Kabre, Losso, Naudemba, Mossi, Tem, Ewe, Watchi, Fulbe, Hausa, Akposso, Adele, Ashanti, Guang, Gurma, Yoruba, Akpafu, Awatime, etc. But it should be noted at this point that these peoples do not belong only to Togoland but are diffused throughout the whole of West Africa. What more is there to be said? Togoland lacks even the old justification for colonialist robbery, that is, mineral wealth, which, apart from a small amount of phosphates, is absent. Probably Togoland owes its existence to an obstinate desire for prestige on the part of Kaiser Wilhelm's Germany which had been excluded from the first stage of the pillaging of Africa. And also to the fact that the German explorer Dr Gustav Nachtigal, in 1884, in agreement with the native chiefs (and who knows what they thought they were doing, either the chiefs or Nachtigal!) proclaimed the German protectorate. In face of such 'historical' justifications, I think it may well be said, with a suitable tautology, that Togoland exists because it exists.

In the light of this tautology, our misadventures at various frontiers during our journey along the Gulf of Guinea acquire a more correct perspective. To tell the truth, we had almost forgotten, during the journey, that African nations existed; the road gave one a feeling, if anything, of infinite space, ignorant and innocent of any kind of arbitrary political frontier. As our car, in a leisurely way but with insatiable appetite, devoured the tens and hundreds of kilometres, everything fled away in front of us, *ad infinitum*: the gloomy, grey sea, the maize-coloured shore, the immensely tall palms segmented like so many thin spinal columns, the track of haemorrhage-red crushed stone, the pale green bush, the sky dimmed by heat-mist. One might well have thought that this monotony and this solitude would never be interrupted. Instead of which, again and again, we had, absurdly, to stop. The road would be closed by a bar like that of a level crossing; a flag would be hanging from a pole; there would be a single-storeyed shanty on one side. On the other side, in the shade of a mango, would be two or three women, motionless in front of a few little tins, a few long loaves of bread, a few piles of red peppers. Then, unhurriedly, in the pause of deep silence that succeeded the hum of our engine, and with the slow, authoritative step characteristic of all the frontier guards in the world, there appeared from the house two or three policemen in shorts and khaki shirts, with epaulettes sewn on to their shirts and the peaks of their caps pulled down over their eyes. Suddenly the infinity of the African continent dissolved like a fleeting mirage. It was replaced by the finiteness of nationality, with the usual, disturbing word: passports.

Now you must know that there were three of us in the car, two of us furnished with Italian passports so that there was no need for a visa; the third, on the other hand, with a passport from another European country needing, alas, all

180

possible visas. I am not concerned with reporting what in any other place but Africa would be considered an abuse, but rather with noting the variety of compromises to which one has recourse in these countries where everything, apart from nature, seems to be provisional and to depend on chance. The following, therefore, were the three solutions that were adopted for the visa problem. The first official, at the first frontier, after a long conversation with our driver, held out his hand to him, and in the course of that cordial, prolonged handshake something like a folded slip of paper passed from the palm of the driver to that of the official: a solution, I should say, of traditional type. At a second frontier, again there were the handshake and the passing of the slip of paper from one palm to the other; but at the last moment – wonderful to relate! – the official called back the driver and gave him back the money: since the foreigner had been forced to travel by car (and therefore to need visas) inasmuch as he had missed his aeroplane, it would not be right to take advantage of his misfortune and so the visa would be given free – a solution, it might be said, existential and of a Dostoevskyan type. And finally the third solution, the most complex and the most articulate of the three. At first the visa was firmly refused. A printed circular was displayed from which it was clear that our friend's country of origin was not amongst those for which no visa was required. A discreet, euphemistic proposal to 'oil the wheels' was rejected with virtuous, almost threatening indignation. In the end, after long discussions, it was suggested that authorization might be asked by telephone from the chief of the local police. But with renewed firmness we were refused permission to make use of the telephone that was part of the equipment of the frontier office: regulations forbade it.

So there we were, under the scorching sun of early afternoon, compelled to go in search of a telephone in the neighbouring village. At that hour the whole place was asleep. Beyond the road that skirted the shore, the grey, metallic sea formed a blinding background to the black silhouettes of the palm-trees and the meditative groups of fishermen squatting on the beach. Finally we discovered the post office in a melancholy little *art nouveau* villa at the end of a sandy garden. We shut ourselves in the call box and telephoned. Awakened, perhaps, from his siesta, the chief of police at first had difficulty in understanding. Then, with sudden cordiality, he assured us that he would telephone to the frontier. We went back. The telephone call had already had its effect. There was a smile of agreement; the passport was lying open on the rickety little table; a long, bony, gnarled hand seized the rubber stamp and imprinted the visa in violet ink. Unexpectedly, however, the passport was not handed over and the zealous official, having made us respect the law, proceeded himself to break it by asking for the money he had refused a little earlier. And so, for the third time, another slip of paper changed hands.

This is the point at which the usual moral reflections might be expected, which, however, I must avoid. I do not, in fact, believe that in such cases as this one should speak of corruption, not at least in any profound sense. It is, if anything, a survival of traditional habits. There are about thirty African nations and they have existed for barely ten years; the tribes, so it seems, amounted and still amount to some thousands and have existed from time immemorial. What did the tribal chiefs formerly do when explorers heedlessly crossed invisible tribal frontiers? They imposed a toll in kind (beads, copper wire, lengths of material, arms) which, however, it must be noted, did not have the character of a genuine tax but rather of a capricious favour on their part and of a rightful homage on the part of the strangers. Thus, probably, can be explained the otherwise mysterious restitution of the money already requested for the second visa. Corruption and the law have often a point in common: that they claim to be the same for everybody. But individual caprice acknowledges the right of existence to individual exceptions.

32

In the Footsteps of Gide

Duala, February 1972

Duala is one of the many towns that have arisen round the Gulf of Guinea during the last twenty years, with an urban development comparable, in rapidity and impetuosity but also in catastrophic indifference to the human problem, only to that of Latin America. Abidjan, Lomé, Cotonu, Accra, Kumasi, Lagos, Ibadan, all of them cities of over a hundred thousand inhabitants, and sometimes even half a million, reflect the colonialism which gave rise to them with the precision and clarity of a sociological manual. The particular kind of trade that is characteristic of colonialism does not succeed, in these towns, even in creating the much to be deprecated 'consumer civilization'; it remains a mere barter of manufactured goods for raw materials. This barter, in turn, places local labour on a level with raw materials. From the interior of these countries, both products and men, coerced by demand, stream into the towns to be exchanged, thanks to the mechanism of prices and wages, for the manufactured goods of the metropolis. The latter, with all the goodwill in the world and even if it does not desire it, especially on the administrative level, cannot help over-exploiting the colony, being forced to do so, in any case, by the fragile character of native culture and the generosity of tropical nature. Sprung up – it is no exaggeration to say so – like a mushroom in the heart of the equatorial forest, at the foot of the immensely high Mount Cameroon which no one has ever seen in its entirety because it is always hidden in the clouds, Duala, damp, sultry and misty, is a typical town of the depressed and depressing

Africa so well described by Céline in his *Voyage au bout de la nuit*, in which the Europeans, liverish and overwhelmed by sand, are forced to live, tied to business or administration, waiting to return as soon as possible, with their savings or their pension, to their native land. It was not, therefore, the Cameroons that caused Duala to spring up; it was not needed and anyhow could not have been supplied by the local village economy; it was, rather, the European metropolis which uninterruptedly unloaded upon it industrial products and then loaded up coffee, cocoa, rubber and bauxite. Exports to France have multiplied the stores and warehouses in the region of the harbour; imports from France, the markets and counting-houses; and these, strung out along shapeless streets, have in the end formed the commercial centre of the town, a criss-cross of urban squalor and feverish traffic. As for the inhabitants, they have distributed themselves in the usual uneven manner typical of colonial towns: the governing class, almost entirely European, in the restricted residential quarter of villas and small houses with gardens; the African proletariat in the *bidonvilles*, *nattavilles* and other scattered groups of dwellings climbing up the steep slopes of red earth amongst the tangled, decrepit green of the surviving strips of the equatorial forest.

We were there in order to organize a journey by car which, following in the footsteps of André Gide, will take us from Duala steadily northwards across the Cameroons to Fort Lamy in the Chad. Gide, in point of fact, made this journey, which he called *Retour du Tchad*, in the opposite direction, from Fort Lamy to Duala; he did it partly on horseback, following the tracks, partly by boat on the rivers, whereas we should do it in a Land-Rover; he took more than two months whereas we, conveniently, should take two weeks. But Duala, it seems, had the same unfavourable effect upon the French writer as it had upon us: 'What an hotel! Better the most odious stage-post. And what whites! Dirt, idiocy, vulgarity!' However it must be observed that perhaps to Gide, who was coming from the still untouched territories of the interior of the Cameroons, Duala, by contrast, may have appeared more squalid than it did to us who arrived by plane.

We made our purchases with a mixed feeling of jocularity and uneasiness. Jocularity because we were pretending that, in order to go from Duala to Fort Lamy, it was necessary to organize one's journey whereas, now, probably one could simply leave one fine morning without making any preparations at all. Uneasiness, because this jocularity was based upon a certain number of exotic, venturesome commonplaces. For in Africa, no sooner has one adopted a certain method of travelling than it becomes immediately a commonplace. First of all there was the terrible reality of exploration; but with time and progress this was transformed into a commonplace worthy of Tartarin de Tarascon. Then came the journey in the manner of Gide, still uncomfortable and dangerous, with horses, boats and caterpillar vehicles; even this way of seeing Africa very soon became merely conventional. Finally there dawned the era of the track and the Land-Rover. Nevertheless the track and Land-Rover, perhaps still necessary and realistic for hunting in the bush, are taking on an appearance of uselessness and commonplace when it is a question of journeys as normal as ours, for which – with a certain amount of risk, it is true – any ordinary car would perhaps suffice. In any case even the word 'track' reveals, if closely examined, a linguistic trick. What in fact is a 'track' if not the old, quiet, unmetalled European road of the period before asphalt?

Anyhow, we went with our list of things to be bought to one of the many emporiums and handed it over to a pale, emaciated French assistant who, after looking through it, went off to find the goods in the chaos of boxes and tins and various packages piled up in the back room behind the shop. Thus we bought the usual tins of corned beef, of sardines in oil, of fruits in syrup of which, at the end of our journey, we should make a present to our driver; the usual medicines that we should abandon, unused, in our last hotel; the thermos flask which, at the first hole in the track, would fall to pieces; the bottles of beer which would be made disgusting and undrinkable by the heat. Then we went to a big transport depot, a kind of little hell of petrol pumps, workshops and car parks in which African mechanics in overalls moved lazily around in the sultry, sunless heat. Here, from the French manager (rotund, pipe in mouth, short sleeves, hairy forearms) we ordered the *tous terrains* Land-Rover with which we intended to face the crags of the high plateau and the grass of the great plain. Then a disaster! Driven for a trial run on the open space of the depot, the Land-Rover, although new, left on the cement a thin, black snake of oil: the tank had been mysteriously damaged. So our journey was postponed for a day and we had to stay at Duala.

We did not stay there. We decided to move to Victoria, a hundred kilometres from Duala in the ex-British Cameroons, an enchanting place, the publicity leaflets assured us, in no way inferior to the famous paradises of the South Seas. We started off by car along the road which goes downhill through forests and plantations all the way to Victoria. It was a useful journey, if only because it allowed a close view of the massacre of Africa. Nothing is more majestic and poetical than the equatorial forest when still untouched ; nothing is sadder and more miserable than the same forest when the trees have been cut down. In the first case the wood is still virgin in the literal sense of the word, that is, absolutely impenetrable, with trees even as much as thirty metres high trailing after them, hanging to their branches, veritable cloaks of lianas and creepers. In the second case, on the other hand, the trees have been felled and here and there in the forest are earthy, red clearings with a few scattered stumps, and one is reminded of a scalp afflicted with alopecia, a disease that causes the hair to fall out in patches, unevenly. Preferable, then, are the plantations, like a kind of vegetable barracks with their rubber trees in military ranks, closely aligned, up and down the slopes. They do, at any rate, bring relative prosperity to the numerous villages through which we passed at intervals. They were villages of huts, with unpaved roads and no drains; but they swarmed with girls and young men dressed in clean, well-pressed clothes, pleasant to look at with their shrill colours against dark complexions.

Then, amongst hills crowned with drooping, swollen vegetation, we came upon a group of English-type cottages nestling at the bottom of a wide, misty valley. The air was more humid and sultry than at Duala; Victoria seemed immersed in the greenish, impure water of an old aquarium. We spoke of our disappointment to our driver, who, French-speaking and therefore a participant, without being aware of it, in the French anti-British controversy, agreed with us and answered sententiously: 'The English, as we all know, do everything wrong. And this, as you see, is the result.'

We left our luggage at the hotel and plunged down by narrow paths, anxious to reach the 'South Seas' promised by the publicity leaflet. Little resemblance to the South Seas, however! There indeed was the sea, down below a decaying terrace: it did not look like the Gulf of Guinea but more like the North Sea round Scotland. A dense, dirty fog hung over the grey, motionless expanse of the waters; countless little wooded islands, vague and half concealed, showed ghostly outlines in the mist. A few fishing-boats, black as pitch, lay at anchor. The bay formed a curve between two foggy promontories, from which, sunk in tropical vegetation of so dark a green as to be almost black, peeped the walls and roofs of decrepit, crumbling colonial habitations. The heat was stifling, the air was dark although it was noon, the sun in the sky was like a piece of round, yellowish spittle. We leant out cautiously to look at the sea, down below the terrace. There were no cliffs, there were no waves; nothing but a crumbling mass of blackish stones half submerged in the stagnating water.

33

Victor and the Elephants

Yaundé, February 1972

Victor, our driver, was a man of under thirty who belonged originally to a tribe whose home was not far from Ngaunderé in the Central Cameroons. He was a tall, strong young man, an athletic type, with long legs and broad shoulders.

Victor had a fine African head, characterized, however, by a kind of caricature-like simplification of feature that made his face look like a mask. His eyes were large and rather ugly, and he had a disturbing tendency to roll them; his nose was short, broad and hooked; his mouth curving, and with a nauseated, scornful expression. The colour of his complexion was dark but not black, so that the scanty, pointed, rather Othello-like beard which Victor allowed to grow during our journey stood out with its coal-blackness against the roast-coffee darkness of his skin. Victor had fine, long hands, strong and lean; sharp, white, wolf-like teeth; a loose-limbed, very light, feline way of walking. And finally his voice: a loud, excessively virile voice, with a perpetually discontented, rancorous, menacing tone.

Victor, until the day before, had been a lorry-driver. In his manner of driving and of estimating distances, one was aware of the hard-working long-distance driver, capable of covering the three thousand kilometres between Duala and Fort Lamy in three days, precisely the same journey that, with us, he would be obliged to perform in two weeks. As a lorry-driver, a desperate devourer of kilometres, Victor had an absolute insensitivity to beauties of landscape and unexpected encounters. Probably our method of travelling must have seemed to him an eccentricity on the part of rather stupid whites, a folly. But we were clients, we paid, and that was enough.

Victor was probably exploited pitilessly during his years of apprenticeship. From that bitter experience, however, he had not derived what is generally called class-consciousness, but rather a firm determination to exploit in his turn. Victor's dream, of which he often spoke to us, was to become rich, setting up on his own with one lorry to begin with and taking thorough advantage of other Victors, other strong, innocent boys who, like him, had arrived straight from the bush. Victor was a Balzac character, a century and a half late; a César Birotteau of the wheel. Perhaps he would succeed in becoming rich. But perhaps the unforeseeable developments of neo-colonialism in Africa would thwart his ambition, would sidetrack it towards different goals.

Victor, a traditionalist by nature, wanted to get married. He told us that, in order to marry, he would have to put aside a hundred thousand francs with which, together with an ox, young and of good weight, he could buy a wife. At first, so it seemed, Victor had thought of finding himself a wife at Duala. But his chief, the French manager of the transport company for which he worked, had dissuaded him from this, explaining that the city girls, having come into contact with town life, did not inspire confidence. Better a girl from his own tribe, a girl not yet spoiled by civilization. Obediently Victor took the advice of his chief, whom his deeply rooted conformism made him look upon as a kind of father; and so, now, in a remote village in the Cameroons, some girl was waiting for Victor to present himself with his hundred thousand francs and his fat ox.

With regard to his chief, Victor's relationship with him was very complex and faithfully reflected Victor's no less complex relationship with the French. Victor was at the mission school and spoke excellent French; obviously he admired the French without reservation, and in some way he separated and distinguished them from the other whites. One day I happened to remark that a certain road might turn out to be impracticable; Victor replied at once, with absolute assurance: 'Impossible, it was made by the French.'

189

Nevertheless, in a curiously contradictory way, Victor, who was always angry and always convinced that he was being swindled, entertained towards the French, side by side with his admiration, a suspicion that, after all, they were exploiters. Leftist propaganda? Or perhaps incipient nationalism? It is difficult to say. But one day Victor astonished me by speaking with contempt of certain *colonialistes* of little importance who, after independence came to the Cameroons, had to leave their more lucrative jobs at Duala for obscure occupations in minor towns in the interior. The fate of these people aroused vindictive sarcasm in Victor.

Victor's ambiguousness with regard to colonialism matched his analogous ambiguousness with regard to religion. Victor was a Catholic, and in a strange, self-satisfied, sombre way was proud of it, but this did not prevent his believing in magic, with a curious mixture of terror and of profound, almost ironic familiarity. The following is a dialogue between us on the subject of magic.

'Victor, you believe in magic?'

'Of course I do. How could one not believe in it? I've had four friends who died through witchcraft.'

'How does this witchcraft work?'

'You go into the witch-doctor's hut, in the dark. You don't see anything or anybody. All you hear is the mysterious voice asking for the name of the person you want to die. If you say the name and do the things the witch-doctor orders you to do, the person mentioned, in the course of a few days, dies.'

'Have you yourself caused anyone to die?'

'No, I haven't. I'm frightened. Besides, it costs a great deal. The witch-doctor wants money, more and more money. When you've fallen into the grip of magic, you can never get out of it.'

'Why? Does the witch-doctor use blackmail?'

'You can never get out of it.'

Victor, furthermore, had not the smallest shade of Christian feeling. He did not love his neighbour as himself; and he regularly did to others what he would not wish to be done to himself. Victor was an unconscious Darwinian; for him, in life, it was the strongest who gained the victory, that is, the most skilful in life itself. This mentality was continually revealed during our journey. Nothing made him laugh more delightedly, with his wolf-like, sarcastic, contemptuous laugh, than a lorry upside down in a ditch, with its wheels in the air. Someone else's misfortune filled him with joy, especially if it was a question of a road accident, because that was a misfortune which, as an ex-lorry driver, he could fully appreciate. That laughter implied: 'Me yesterday, you today.' Moreover Victor was extremely harsh with the many wayfarers who, in these wild solitudes, would ask for a lift. For instance, as we were driving along the track over a boundless plain of tall grass an old man, white-haired, his face shrunken with fatigue, with a bundle on his head and a spear in his hand, made an imploring signal to us. We told Victor to stop and take him on board the car. He obeyed unwillingly; and then, as he drove on, he became enraged with the old man, finding fault with him for dirtying 'his' Land-Rover with his sandals covered with sand; for breaking 'his' windows with the iron tip of his spear. At that moment Victor was identifying himself with his transport company and defending its property. When the old man got out, gratefully and humbly thanking us, Victor merely threw his spear out on to the ground with a look of contempt.

Or, again, there was the unlucky young lorry-driver, standing in the midday sun beside his lorry which was overturned in the ditch. We picked him up. Victor immediately asked him how much he earned; as soon as he heard, he started raging at him, sarcastically and cruelly: it was a starvation wage; he would die in poverty, he and his family; he would never succeed in bettering his own condition; he was a beast of burden, a servant, a slave. The young man defended himself as best he could; but Victor gave him no respite. And during the whole time we had him in the car he went on predicting a catastrophic future for him.

The only time I saw Victor show any feeling that was not one of bitterness or contempt was in relation to the wild animals of Africa. I remember a day when we had stopped in front of a clearing which was all trampled down and marked with colossal footprints. The trees and bushes were shattered and leafless; and enormous lumps of excrement, cubic in shape, were scattered here and there. The elephants could not be far away. And indeed, when we had got out of the car and had started walking through the bush, we saw the great beasts surrounded by a great cloud of dust, marching off towards some unknown, distant feeding-ground or shelter. The dust enveloped them; but through the haze could be distinguished the outlines of their trunks, of their tusks, of their heads with their great ears; and, close against the enormous legs of their mothers, the young ones, elegant and massive. From time to time there would be a few melancholy, strident trumpetings from the herd. Then I saw Victor laughing nervously and anxiously as he ran towards the elephants, with feet so light that they seemed not even to touch the ground. As he ran he waved his arms, as if to call the elephants back and make them understand that he wanted them to wait for him, because he wished to join them and walk with them through the bush. At that moment Victor, without being conscious of it, seemed to express the longing of the African for the Africa of the time before the colonial invasion, the Africa of the village and the great plains of which, when with us, he spoke with so much contempt.

34

Irregular Vegetable Life

Yaundé, March 1972

In *Rêve Parisien*, Baudelaire imagined a fantastic city of metal, marble and water. From this dream city, which anticipated the very latest solutions for urban development, Baudelaire tells us that *végétal irrégulier* was banished. What does this mean? That Baudelaire's city was rational, from beginning to end, and that 'irregular vegetable life' was banished from it precisely because its irregularity was synonymous with irrationality. But what is reason if not the wholly mental activity which distinguishes man from nature? And so we come to the essential point of the question: Baudelaire's city was solely human, that is rational, without any concession to irrationality, that is to nature.

Now in African villages the exact opposite happens to what happens in Baudelaire's city. 'Regular' metal and stone are banished; the only material used is 'irregular' vegetable life. Moreover this material is not transformed into posts and beams and other wooden elements, all of them alike, as happens in countries where products of the forests are industrialized, but is transferred almost without modification from the forest to the village. Hence some strange effects. For example, the look of decrepitude in the villages: stone and metal do not age; vegetable matter does. Or rather, stone and metal do not live; vegetable matter lives and therefore dies. The African village, formed of straw and reeds, of boughs and leaves and tree-trunks, appears to be built of a material that is not so much transformed as dead, a material which, like everything that is dead, retains, in a menacing sort of way, some appearance of life.

African villages, especially those in the mountainous or prairie zones (in the rain forest, alas, there are now a number of timber-yards) are bizarre, disquieting, bewitched places. One drives through fifty or a hundred or two hundred kilometres of wildly monotonous bush country, devoid of any kind of life except that of trees; then, all of a sudden, in an unexpected clearing, there is a village. It is surrounded by an enclosing wall which in reality is a single very long piece of matting supported by posts at irregular intervals. Behind this enclosing wall of vegetable matter, in some places sagging and decaying, in some places erect and tightly stretched, there appear, jammed one against the other and looking like cone-shaped mushrooms, the thatched roofs of the huts. There is no one to be seen; not a sound to be heard. Just two or three threads of dark smoke rise from the roofs towards the brilliant, improbably blue sky; a few monkeys leap among the branches of the trees which form a background to the clearing; a thin, yellow dog lies in the open space in front of the huts, apparently dead.

But if human life seems to be lacking, vegetable life, to make up for it, continues, bizarre, malignant. On top of the roofs, forked sticks protrude, suggesting ideas of torture; the posts that support the matting are, in reality, small trees recently lopped, with bristling spikes that had been branches and crooked shafts that had been trunks. These forks and spikes are dead, they have the colour of dry wood, brown or yellow; but, just because they are dead, they conjure up, threateningly, the bush where once they were alive. The same can be said of the ground round the village: it is not paved or asphalted, it is exactly the same ground as that of the forest, deprived, it is true, of its mosses, of its creepers, of its dead leaves; but it is not really transformed. We turned off the engine and stopped to look, scarcely daring to take the customary photographs. Then, in the enclosing wall of matting, a little door, also of matting, opened and a woman appeared holding a baby. She had a piece of bright-coloured material wound round her body, from her breast down to her ankles, and on her head a big turban of the same material, shaped like a cauliflower. The little girl was completely naked save for a string of blue beads round her loins. They looked at us for a moment, without moving; and, during that moment, one almost thought that they too were a part of the lifelessness of the place. Not at all, however; suddenly they both smiled broadly, showing very white teeth, and held out hands asking, as happened everywhere, for money in exchange for the taking of their picture. Then suddenly I understood that the irrationality of nature, as expressed in the bewitched air of the village, was hostile not only to us but to them too. And that the village, in its way and relatively to the violent irrationality of tropical nature, was also an illusion of rationality, the most austere that was possible in Africa, like Baudelaire's city.

These reflections found confirmation in the forest, a few days later. We were in the Central Cameroons, below the Adamaua massif, and the road map showed a waterfall in a river at a particular point. We decided to go there. We left the track and drove along a narrow path through tall, very thick grass which pressed upon us on all sides and prevented our seeing anything but the sky. We went bumping along for about ten kilometres; then we came out into a clearing made by foresters where the ground was broken up and weedy, and littered with tree-trunks already cut up and thrown here and there, and with huge stumps. The whole of one side of the clearing was blocked by the dark tangle of the forest. We listened carefully and, in the absolute silence, there came to us, unmistakably, the subdued, distant roar of the waterfall.

Then we started off again, still following the path which plunged straight into the forest. We were going forward now almost in darkness, with the rustling foliage rubbing against the sides of the Land-Rover and sometimes actually penetrating into it through the windows. The slopes of dried mud left over from the rainy season became both higher and deeper, and the car could go no further; we got out and made our way on foot. The path was now a veritable tunnel hollowed out through the thickness of the foliage; everywhere there were lianas, dangling from above like snakes, from which one drew back in fear to see whether they ended in traingular heads with forked tongues; even on the ground they were so snake-like that one avoided treading on them; or they would be reaching up and up with a spiral movement, as though in flight. The rain forest enclosed us on all sides, silent, quivering. As one's eye became accustomed to this darkness full of green vegetation, it became gradually possible to distinguish the various levels of arboreal structure: a first level of ferns and other plants of the undergrowth; a second, of shrubs; a third, of small trees such as are to be seen in a coppice; a fourth, of trees of normal height; finally a fifth, of giants of thirty or fifty metres in height. The lianas twist and twine among these different levels, like living vegetable ladders; each level has its own floor of foliage; superimposed one on another, the platforms of leaves finally obstruct the passage of light.

We came at last to a small clearing into which, from high above, fell a ray of sunshine like those dusty, filtered rays that penetrate the stained-glass windows of cathedrals. The roar of the waterfall was now close by; and a kind of sloping hole, going down through the thick of the forest, appeared to lead to the bank of a river. But it was necessary to crawl almost on hands and knees; so I myself gave up and remained alone while my companions went on through the foliage. On a branch I saw a single yellow flower; I went forward to pick it; the flower flew away – it was a butterfly. But then I made a discovery; behind the curtain of shrubs, in the dense shadow, all of a sudden I caught sight of the base of an enormous tree. It had the shape, the consistency, the movement of a muscle, of one of the muscles that join the shoulder to the neck and that tighten if you turn and bend your head towards your shoulder. It was a gigantic muscle, of dark green, covered with smooth, soft bark which was even, perhaps, warm, and which looked like skin. The tree made one think of a man buried up to his armpits and who, in place of a head, had a perfectly straight tapering trunk, like a vertiginous thorn rising up and up, undaunted, till its point was lost in the green mist of the highest levels of the forest.

This colossal muscle formed a kind of dark cave, impenetrable to the eye and which might also contain some feline animal lying in wait or a hibernating snake. I preferred to think, however, that in spite of the industrial deforestation, the spirit of the forest still dwelt in that cave – that hideous, odd divinity for centuries represented by the animist Africans in fetishes with grave, ironical expressions, or again in terrifying masks with smiles made of beads and eyes of raffia. It was to this spirit that nature dedicated the cathedral of the rain forest. And, just as sacred furnishings placed as ornaments in a drawing-room nevertheless retain something of their religious flavour, so does this spirit persist in the malignant, crooked shapes of the branches and tree-trunks that serve as supports for the huts, impregnating the African village with the air of bewitchment that is so striking to the European traveller.

The legends and fables of Europe often allude to this spirit: the horror of the woods, the fear of being lost in the forest, the terror of the tree that does not speak, that does not move, and yet is alive. But the European, accustomed by now not only to Baudelaire's marble and metal but also to plastics and other synthetic materials, should come here to Africa to feel again, if only for a single instant of irrational alarm, its disquieting presence.

I awoke from these reflections at a rustling sound of disturbed foliage. It was my companions returning, disappointed. They had not succeeded in reaching the river. And, while they were on their way, even the sound of the waterfall had entirely ceased.

35

The Nymphs of the Cameroons

Rey Buba, March 1972

Usually, during a journey, a stranger feels uncertain and uneasy because he does not know the men and the places where he is and is afraid of making mistakes and getting lost. The native, on the other hand, who accompanies him as guide or friend, is at ease, with the assurance of someone who moves in a familiar setting. Not so in Africa, however; at least not in our case. A lion when at a short distance from towns, our driver Victor turned into a rabbit in the bush country which he surely ought to have known well, seeing that he was born there. Solitudes troubled him; road junctions distressed him; the state of the road surface worried him. Often I was on the point of saying to him: 'After all, why such cautiousness? It's your own country, you ought to know it.' But then I restrained myself, reflecting that he was worried and frightened precisely because he knew the country well. We foreigners, on the other hand, having confidence in the road map and in the engine of the Land-Rover, were serene and trustful just because we knew nothing of Africa.

In Africa the principal tracks run across districts in which – although with differences owing to the natural surroundings – one can recognize a historical tempo not dissimilar from that of Europe. Lorries, motels, petrol pumps, telegraph offices, schools, police and so on, all go to show that even here it is the year 1972, more or less. But leaving the principal track and turning aside into a secondary track often means taking a backward leap of centuries into feudal and barbaric, or actually prehistoric, situations. These backward leaps over the centuries are exciting. Anyone who has seen, in the bush, a boy hunting rabbits and bending his bow in exactly the same manner as the archers in Assyrian bas-reliefs, or, beneath the battle-mented walls of a Sudanese town, a caracoling horseman armed with sword and spear, will become aware that his journey is far more in time than in space, and that in Africa all that is needed is a river or a small chain of mountains to transport him from the modern world to the Middle Ages or the Bronze Age.

But it is precisely these backward leaps in time that frighten our driver Victor. Having been born in the bush, he has a feeling of repugnance for primitive animism and magic; Islamic feudalism, moreover, perhaps awakens in him an atavistic memory of the slave raids. What he likes is the modern world, with its cars and its lack of mystery. Therefore when, at a road junction, I told him that we must turn to the right and make for the town of Rey Buba, he looked at me in astonishment: 'Why Rey Buba? We're supposed to be going to Fort Lamy. For Fort Lamy we have to turn to the left.'

I could not tell him that I wished to go to Rey Buba because André Gide, in his diary, quoted the following remark from a letter from Captain Coste: 'The Sultan of Rey Buba is the owner of all the wealth of all men.' He would not understand me, he would think I was mad. So, seeing that cultural curiosity would seem to him a mere caprice, I said to myself that it would be just as well to justify myself by means of naked, crude, authoritarian caprice, which perhaps would be more acceptable to him. I said curtly: 'We want to go to Rey Buba. Why? There's no "why" about it. It just *is* so.'

This discussion took place at midday, after a lonely drive of about a hundred kilometres, at a cross-roads hemmed in on all sides by tall, very thick grass. There was nothing to be seen but the sky, whitened by heat mist, in which a few black vultures were slowly circling. There was, it is true, a crooked signpost with an arrow and the name Rey Buba; but such was the solitude that even that seemed unreal. Victor insisted: 'This isn't a track. You can scarcely see it because of the grass. We shall end up goodness knows where.'

'It's marked on the map, anyhow.'

'It's not marked with a red sign nor even with a red-and-white dotted line. It's only white.'

'But, Victor, you know perfectly well that in Africa there are only two kinds of road: asphalt roads and those that aren't asphalted.'

He said nothing, but put the car into gear and furiously drove the Land-Rover through the grass. We went forward like a motor-boat cleaving tall breakers in a rough sea. The grass was indeed like waves: it opened in front of the bonnet and then immediately closed in again behind the boot. The track was in reality a path for cattle which had left excrement everywhere, still damp and glossy on the dusty ground. I said to Victor, to reassure him: 'Cows have been going along here. Where a cow can go, the Land-Rover can go.'

Silently, in a rage, he went on driving, making gestures of discontent and apprehension. We proceeded for about ten kilometres. Finally Victor broke his silence, pointing at the dashboard with his long bony finger: 'We have petrol enough for only twenty kilometres more, at most.'

'Soon the grass will come to an end and we shall reach a village.'

'There aren't any villages.'

As though deliberately, the path suddenly emerged from the grass and we were confronted by a limitless plain where the grass had already been burned, according to the custom of the season. Black with burning, with brown streaks of earth and, here and there, the charred skeletons of shrubs, the plain stretched away to the horizon, malignant, scorched, utterly deserted. As often happens in Africa, one sees the traces of man but not man himself. The peasants obviously had burnt the grass of the prairie, but, however much one looked around, there was no sign of habitations. Victor remarked sardonically: 'Where is the village?'

Somewhat irritated, I replied: 'Look at those three or

four dark balloons, over there on the horizon. Those are mango-trees. And mangoes, at any rate in this part of the Cameroons, are inseparable from villages. Where there are mangoes, there are villages.'

He did not appear convinced; but he went on. We crossed the charred plain and, in the end, I was able to have my own modest triumph. The dark, spherical lumps of the mango foliage became more precise, and round them, cowering in their shade, appeared the huts. A few minutes more, and we were in the open space of a village. In the shade of the mangoes were the usual groups of women squatting in front of minute piles of fruit and tubers for sale, the usual swollen-bellied children silently playing, the usual donkey with its front feet tied together to prevent it escaping, hopping from place to place to nibble the grass in the ditch. The huts were surrounded by the usual wall of matting and the usual sugarloaf roofs peeped out above it. We called to a boy; a dozen of them ran up to us. Victor spoke to them in the language of his tribe, from the neighbourhood of Yaundé, but the boys, alas, for all their zealous goodwill, did not understand him. One of them, however, beckoned to me understandingly and invited me to follow him. I got down from the car and walked behind him along vague, sandy paths among the huts. An old, old woman, bent double with age (her long, flat breasts dangled in the air) opened the little door of a hut and with a great effort pulled out a basket covered with a white cloth sewn on to the wickerwork. She cut the stitching and extracted . . . a parcel of English-type bread wrapped in cellophane. Nigerian bread, probably, which had reached this village by who knows what succession of lorries and donkeys. However I bought the bread, of which there is always a need, and went back to the car. There, during my brief absence, a providential thing had occurred: a white man had come by in a car and had provided information about a petrol pump. We started off again.

We were again right in the midst of what I hate most in Africa, bush country. Better the desert, which is at least truly dead; better the great plain, intoxicating, anyhow, in its monotony. The bush is alive but in a mediocre sort of way, like an interminable nursery-garden of trees which never manages to become a forest; it is monotonous but without order, it is shapeless, chaotic. Despairingly we inspected millions of trees; then, unexpectedly, we had our reward: the bush thinned out, then ceased, and we found ourselves in open country, on damp soil, amongst green, shining plants. Not far away we could see a wide, majestic, lonely mirror of dark, motionless water, a great river. Its bank was strewn with enormous black rocks piled up as though by some giants' game. An oval rock, the largest of all, was balanced on top of the pile and made one feel it had been there since prehistoric times, the thousand-years-old erosions of which, in its perfection, it recalled. On the other bank of the river, great heavy-foliaged trees were disposed in a picturesque, romantic manner, as in a picture by Poussin or Claude Lorrain. The trees stood guard over a small, grassy beach upon which, as in paintings of mythological subjects, one expected to see the little white figure of a naked nymph. But we were in Africa, and natural solitudes there are populated by wild animals, the last in the world, hippopotamuses, giraffes, lions, antelopes, elephants. These are the real flesh-and-blood nymphs, who have taken refuge in these deserted places to represent the true aspect of the innocent mystery, the timeless happiness of which the nymphs of classical mythology were the symbolical expression. Even here, in this nameless river, there was no lack of a nymph. The nymph had an enormous cylindrical body, short, crooked legs like a dachshund, a great head, fit for a carnival mask, in the shape of a shoe. It was a hippopotamus. Unaware that we were watching him, he emerged from the shady beach, came out on to the bank, hesitated, then slid down and disappeared into the river, noiselessly, without ruffling the smooth, black surface of the water. There followed a long, profound silence. Then a spurt of water, a long distance from the beach, revealed the presence of the huge submerged animal. And now the periscope-like eyes, the little ears like those of a horse, part of the thick-skinned back appeared above the surface. A strange, rather strident whinnying sound, like air bursting violently forth from a narrow vent, was answered by another and then another. More backs and more periscopes emerged from the mirror-like water. The nymphs were bathing.

36

Fires and Tomtoms

In his *Retour du Tchad* André Gide thus describes his arrival
at Rey Buba, seat of the Sultan Fulbé: 'And already there
could be seen advancing towards us twenty-five men on
horseback, of bizarre, dark, sober aspect; only when they
came near did I understand that they were wearing coats
of mail of burnished steel, their heads covered with helmets
surmounted by strange crests.' Gide, in this description,
tells us two things: firstly, that at Rey Buba he had a
solemn reception, worthy of his importance as a semi-
official personage from the metropolis travelling in the
colony. Secondly, that the small mountain-range that
separates the territory of the Sultan of Rey Buba from the
rest of the Cameroons also divides, in this part of Africa,
the modern world from the Middle Ages.

I am not, alas, a semi-official personage; and in any case,
theoretically at least, neither metropolis nor colony any
longer exists. And so, on my arrival at Rey Buba, I was
welcomed only by the usual yellow, hungry dogs which, at
the approach of our car, rose with an effort from the dust
in which they were lying, as though dead, in the middle of
the road. But possibly it was this entrance without fanfares
that allowed me, more so than Gide, to become aware of
the dry odour of the centuries which had remained enclosed
within the clay walls of this town.

And there, in the meantime, was the first antiquity: the
bridge made of matting. We saw it from the top of a slope
on to which we had come out after one of our usual desperate
drives through the bush. We could see a wide river-bed

traversed by streaks of stagnant greenish water, by tongues of grey sand and low mounds of white pebbles; and stretched across the river a tawny-coloured carpet linking the two banks. This was a piece of matting; the same matting that in the villages is used as an enclosing wall, supported by poles. All in one piece, variegated with geometrical designs and resting on wooden cross-bars, it crosses the river into the town, of which, behind crumbling, dusty walls, could be seen the sugarloaf roofs and the dark balloons of mango-trees. Who knows when Rey Buba will have a modern bridge, of cement, of iron, of stone, even of wood? And as the car rolled softly over the matting I could not help wondering: 'What do they do in the rainy season? Do they roll up the matting and carry it away, like a circus mat as soon as the show is over? Or do they leave it under water and make a new one?'

We came into Rey Buba at sunset, the sun low on the horizon and lengthening the shadows. The town appeared deserted; after going from street to street and from one group of huts to another, we came out at last into a big square in front of the Sultan's palace. The palace was in Sudanese style, the style half military, half barbaric, like stage scenery, of the monuments of Islamic Africa: slanting walls of dried mud, with battlements and loop-holes; a doorway with a corrugated matting roof and pillars of tree-trunks without bark or branches. In the shadow of the porch two or three guards were sitting on the ground, their swords across their knees; in a corner, leaning against the wall, were a few spears and scimitars, like those in an ancient guard-room. The setting sun cast the shadows of the battlements on to the square and, farther off, the shadow of a solitary child, completely naked, standing there motion-less, looking at us. We took some photographs: the guards did not move; but as soon as we approached the doorway, one of them held out his hand as if telling us to keep away. A confused hum of voices made us turn round. Across the square, from the end of the street, advanced a group of women. There must have been about ten of them, all of them bare to the waist, with pieces of material tied round their hips; each of them was carrying a big basket on her head. As we approached them, they quickened their step in fright. The baskets contained victuals: fruit, tubers, millet, bread, quarters of mutton or goat's flesh, the provisions, evidently, for the supper of the Sultan and his court. But the women hurrying towards the doorway, their bare, prominent breasts tinged with red light by the declining sun, their eyes fixed upon the guards who had now lazily risen from the ground to watch them coming, their hands on their hips – these women brought to mind a servile act of feudal homage that had been repeated every evening for centuries and always in the same manner. As the guide-book to Central Africa euphemistically says: 'Rey Buba, ancient fortified town, celebrated for its Sultan. It still today retains many medieval customs.'

At Rey Buba there was nowhere to sleep; so we went thirty kilometres farther on, to Cholliré, another town in the Sultan's territory where, it seemed, there was a motel. We found it, in fact, outside the town, on a completely flat expanse of ground where the gigantic baobabs seemed to be strategically set out like the pieces on a chess-board. The motel consisted of a big round pavilion with a conical thatched roof. We could have a bedroom; our driver could sleep in the bar-room. After we had eaten by the light of a paraffin lamp we went out into the open; and then we saw that the whole night was aflame with fires blazing all round the horizon. It was the tall grass that the peasants were burning to clear the land for the approaching seed-time. The night was reddened by the fires, and strange black shadows, some moving, some motionless, showed up against the light. Then, as we looked at the fires, the tomtoms started. It seemed, curiously, that the deep, regular beat of the drums, coming from some hidden place, accompanied and kept time with the rhythm of the flames: a thud of tom-toms and tongues of fire leaping high; another thud of tom-toms and the flames dying down again. We asked our driver where they were sounding the tomtoms. He replied laconically that there was a *festa* in Cholliré. We decided to go there.

The *festa* was taking place in darkness, in the square in

which the Sultan's palace was situated, a palace very similar to the one at Rey Buba, even though smaller. The same battlemented walls, the same porch with the roof of matting and tree-trunk columns. The big open space was black with a compact crowd of people, who at first sight seemed to have gathered there for the simple enjoyment of being crushed together. Then the sound of the tomtom gradually emerged from the confused hum of the crowd, imposing its own deep, monotonous, meditative beat, as of a voice murmuring a litany to itself. We made our way through the people to one of the tomtoms. There we saw an old man banging his hands against the ends of a cylindrical drum which he carried hung round his neck; and there were two young men striking the palms of their hands on two drums placed upright on the ground. The crowd formed a circle round them, motionless, all eyes wide open and intent. Then suddenly, as though driven by an irresistible impulse, one of the crowd moved forward and started to dance. He had not made this decision, one felt, because he felt any desire to do so; but because the tomtom, magically, had forced him to it, almost against his will. This perhaps explains the incredible endurance of the dancers who go on moving their feet for hours in accordance with this frenzied, obsessive rhythm. They do not 'wish' to dance, they 'have' to dance; the tomtom has bewitched them and there is nothing to be done about it; victims of a spell, they cannot *not* dance, their faces shining and streaming with sweat and stamped with expressions of fatigue and distress. It would in fact be interesting to know what relationship there is between the monotony of the tomtom and that of the natural African environment. Perhaps it would not be entirely arbitrary to establish a relationship between the infinite repetition of the dunes in the desert, of the acacias in the prairie, of the shrubs in the grassland and this monotony of the drums. Certainly their effect is the same: the detail of the landscape, repeated over and over again for hours and for days, in the end, like the sound of the tomtom, causes a suspension of the mental processes, an intoxicated stupor of the senses.

207

On our way back to bed I noticed two women who were sitting motionless in the dark on the back seats of the Land-Rover, and who did not give us any greeting. They were dressed from breast to ankles in the usual bright-coloured materials; their heads were wrapped in the usual cauliflower-shaped turbans. They seemed young and prepossessing; our driver explained their presence confusedly, saying in an embarrassed way that they were 'friendly' persons. Then, something in their inert, apathetic attitudes reminded me of something else and all of a sudden I realized what kind of 'friendliness' the driver had alluded to. The recollection was of the two courtesans in the picture by Carpaccio who wait, in equally inert and apathetic attitudes, on a balcony in Venice, in expectation of clients. And indeed, when we went into the motel, our driver plunged into the darkness of the bar-room grasping one of the women by the nape of the neck, like a cat. The other one disappeared in company with the custodian.

Later in the night I was suddenly awakened by the sound of subdued chattering. I got up and peered cautiously into the bar-room. There was moonlight, cold and funereal. I seemed instantly to detect, on the driver's bed, an enormous beetle with eight coal-black legs sticking out from under the snow-white, rumpled sheet, four at the head of the bed and four at the bottom. Then, at a second look, I perceived, there on the pillow, four eyes staring at me, wide open. I went back into my room.

37

Naked in the Mountains

Rumsiki, April 1972

We were in a landscape of ruins. Not, however, the ruins of
buildings erected by man, but the ruins of natural elements
which in some remote epoch had attained a final shape of
their own. The mountains were ruins of mountains, with
bare, rust-coloured slopes all crumbling; with peaks that
looked like tumble-down fortresses. The gorge which winds
among these mountain ruins is also the ruin of a gorge
because it is obstructed every now and then by colossal
boulders which have rolled down – there is no knowing
when or from where – and which force the track to make
tortuous circuits. Even the stream that winds along the
bottom of the gorge is a ruin inasmuch as it is dry, except
for traces of black, muddy puddles which reveal the recent
presence of water. Amongst all these ruins, strange,
enormous rocks, smooth and oblong, scattered here and
there, suggest that some gigantic prehistoric bird, after
hovering for a little, had deposited its eggs there and then
flown away without hatching them.

Then the track started to climb, still twisting and turning
along the narrow gorge; and finally it came out into open
air, like the air of a high mountain. Beyond the track, in
the clear sky, and as though slowly coming up out of an
empty abyss, there appeared a whole amphitheatre of
pinnacles and great towers, of castles and cathedrals made
of rock, all tinged with red by the setting sun. These were
the Kapsiki Mountains, an exact copy of our own Dolomites, so like those famous mountains of ours that, for a
moment, we had an illusion that we were not in Africa but

in the Alps, at some viewpoint in the region of Cortina or Carezza.

But Africa does not allow itself to be so easily forgotten. All of a sudden, behind us, a sing-song voice, in soft, quavering French, gave us this information: '*Monsieur*, in front of you are the Kapsiki Mountains. They are called Mount Zivi, Mount Rumchi, Mount Guilli. Over there, beyond, you can see the Mandara mountain-range.' I turned and saw a young woman who smiled broadly at me, with teeth of a dazzling whiteness. She was athletic-looking, Junoesque; she had very broad shoulders, a sculpturesque bosom, powerful arms; and, on top of a muscular, towering neck, a small head with no forehead and no back to it, with a close cap of tiny, tight curls. Behind her, like an opera chorus, stood a group of women, some of them young, others decrepit, a couple of them with babies attached to the longer of their two breasts, the one used for suckling. The sight of these half-naked women and the realization that I was not in the Dolomites but in the north of the Cameroons was one and the same thing. For a European, in fact, mountains are inseparable from the idea of thick, heavy clothing. So that these ebony bosoms whose glossy skin acquired no goose-flesh from the faint breeze that blew softly from the precipice where we were standing, at once dispelled the mental habit of considering mountains as cold places. Pointing to the remote, misty bottom of the valley below us, I asked the young woman who had spoken to me: 'And down there, what is there down there?'

'Nigeria.'

'Nigeria? And what are the Nigerians like?'

'We of the Cameroons don't get on well with the Nigerians.'

'Why is that?'

'Because the Nigerians love quarrelling (*la bagarre*) whereas we of the Cameroons are peaceful people.'

She smiled; then added: 'You want to take a photograph of us?'

'Yes, let us take one.'

'D'you want to see the village?'

'Let's go there.'

'In the village there are the blacksmiths. I'll show them to you.'

'Yes, let us see them.'

'But you'll give me something?'

'Certainly I will.'

But alas! Once I had taken the photograph, surrounded, or rather almost overwhelmed, by the group of women, as I was making my way towards the village behind the athletic young woman with the small head, I realized that, at the moment when the photograph had been taken, I had been attacked by fleas. I felt them jumping between my shirt and my skin; and then I felt them biting me, with all the ferocity of which a flea is capable when it is accustomed to piercing skins inured to exposure to sun and rain and wind and therefore harder than mine. So, as I followed my guide along a very narrow uphill path between two rows of cactuses, I started scratching myself, at first discreetly and with only one hand, then more frankly and with both hands. Then I noticed that a group of urchins following us at a distance had started to mimic me, scratching themselves with exactly the same gestures as mine, as though they were a reflection of me in a mirror. Irritated by the fleas and this teasing, I turned and scolded them vigorously: 'Stop it, leave me in peace, go away!' I expected that they would either give me an angry reply or that they would obey. Not at all: neither one nor the other. In sing-song voices, they repeated: 'Stop it, leave me in peace, go away.' I held up my hand threateningly. The boy immediately behind me repeated the same gesture to the boy behind him and he in turn to the one following him and so on, right down the single file of urchins on that very narrow path. They were, in short, disobeying me and mocking me not in an active way, by attacking me; but in a passive way, by echoing and reflecting me. And there was a touch of sarcasm and buffoonery in their behaviour, of parody, in fact, such as exists in any kind of imitation, especially if it is faithful and unemotional. And so, once again, I had to acknowledge the existence of a sense of humour, always of the same type, which is curiously widespread over the whole of Black

211

Africa, which is strange and archaic, rustic and slightly sinister, a little like the native and patronal deities that seem all the more terrifying, the more smiling and benign they are.

Then we visited the village, a swarm of huts with roofs like skull-caps, camouflaged among rocks and little fields the size of handkerchiefs. As we went from one group of huts to another, out of the little doors, little by little and, it seemed, inexhaustibly, there appeared women, men and children in great numbers, who had been squatting in the darkness of their minute dwellings. And what is the idea that comes to mind on seeing these naked black bodies coming out into the open, into the cramped courtyards of red earth? It is the idea of nudity; the idea that nudity and the hut are made for one another. What I mean to say is that the man who lives in a hut fully dressed, as happens in so many countries in Asia, has to resign himself to dirt because the hut is made of mud and is built on mud. The mats, the robes, the trousers, the turbans, and so on, of some Asiatic peoples are always threadbare and dusty. The only solution to the problem of living in a hut is nudity. Naked like ebony or bronze in his hut, the African is surrounded by objects which are also naked: pottery vessels, iron implements, wooden stools.

Again next day I was made to think of nudity, when we stopped at a cross-roads whence the track – or rather, the mule-path full of stones and pot-holes – branched off across the mountainous country of the Matakam and led to the plain. As we were seeking to trace out this route on the road map, all of a sudden an entire family, completely naked, issued from a little cavern half hidden by the trees. And not merely naked, but also dishevelled, with hair standing on end, suggesting, as it were, the idea of the demented nudity that can sometimes be seen in lunatic asylums. The whole family, laughing frenziedly, threw themselves upon the car, offering for sale some little pipes made of chalk, of their own manufacture and decidedly phallic in form. I noticed that their nakedness was made visible, so to speak, by their ugliness: they all had swollen paunches, with navels that stuck out like the plugs of a barrel; below their paunches, their legs were thin and wrinkled and stiff; the women's breasts were flabby and drooping – all of them things that were only noticeable, one might say, because they were ugly. And so, as I looked at them, I realized that beauty is a kind of clothing; in other words, that a beautiful body is never truly naked. It is probable that nervous disorder, which in the so-called primitive peoples is just as severe (or even more so) as in the so-called civilized, expresses itself in ugliness; whereas beauty goes to indicate an absence of neuroticism.

The mule-track twisted back and forth and up and down through a bizarre, bewitched region, all rocks and villages camouflaged among the rocks, making one think of old paintings representing the Thebaids of the East. Then, at a bend in the track, there suddenly opened wide below us a boundless plain, yellow and green and thickly dotted with dark shrubs. This was the prairie, ante-room of the desert, stretching, uniform and without relief, all the way to Libya.

38

The Market at Fort Lamy

Fort Lamy, April 1972

The Chari is a big African river which at Fort Lamy is extremely wide and almost motionless, like a lake, between low, bare banks, putting one in mind, in the subdued sunset light, of the immense pupil of an eye, dim and dark and destitute of eyelash or eyebrow. I sat in the hotel garden, on the river bank, and looked at the huge red disc of the sun hanging over the opposite shore, so close that it seemed one could touch it. The black silhouette of a dug-out canoe with a man rowing, exactly like some prehistoric rock painting, glided over the water, across the sun. How beautiful they are, these African rivers! Rivers with banks that are, so to speak, non-existent, along which, in perspective, the water seems to merge with the sky; apathetic, deep, thoughtful rivers. The rivers of the hippopotamus: by day these great innocent beasts lie there soaking, only the periscopes of their eyes and the rough hide of their backs emerging from the water; by night, they move up easily on to the banks and go off grazing amongst the papyrus and reed beds, by the light of the moon, herbivorous night-walkers, family by family, the male, the female, one or two young ones, all in order of tonnage, nevertheless mild and peaceful as little goats.

But then the Special Correspondent of an illustrated magazine came over to me. He too had been sitting for some time on the terrace, facing the river; but he was not looking at the sunset, he was looking at me. Finally he could not bear it any longer; he took up his glass and his

bottle of beer and moved over to my table. 'We have alr
met this morning. Will you allow me?'

'Please.'

'Are you going to Tibesti?'

'I should have liked to, but it can't be done: there's
guerrilla trouble.'

The Special Correspondent was small, with a big,
bespectacled head and hair running backwards like that of
someone who looks at the landscape from the window of a
moving train. Triumphantly he retorted: '*I* shall be going
there. I know a French colonel, I shall get the permit. If I
don't get it, I shall go to Tripoli; I know Gaddafi, and I
shall come back from Libya to Zuar. What d'you think of
the Chad?'

'I scarcely know it. I arrived yesterday from the
Cameroons.'

'A very interesting country, the Chad. A racial hybrid, a
criss-cross of interests. An amphibious country: either all
water or all sand. A country divided between Islamized
Africans and Christian Africans. At present it's the latter
who have the upper hand, supported, of course, by the
French. And so the Islamized Africans are carrying on
anti-Imperialist and Nationalist guerrilla warfare.'

'Is it serious, the guerrilla warfare?'

'There are bands of up to two or three hundred men.
Guess who's supporting them.'

'I wouldn't know.'

'In the first place, of course, Libya. But also – you
wouldn't believe it – West Germany.'

'You don't say so!'

'It is so, precisely. Arms and materials. And you know
why?'

'No.'

'The uranium of the Niger, near here, owing to which the
French have created a veritable city in the desert. In fact,
it's the usual thing: an Imperialist struggle. If Tumbalbaye
went, the whole system of the alliance with France would
collapse. That's why France is generous with help . . .'

'Who are the leaders of the guerrillas?'

'Those who fight or those who pull the strings? These latter, in my opinion, are all here at Fort Lamy. And I've got to see them, even if I have to stay here a month. It's a positive mine of news, Fort Lamy. All you have to do is dig, and the news comes spurting out, like the oil in the desert. But if you don't dig, everything seems normal, peaceful, calm.'

At this point the Special Correspondent started to get wildly agitated, waving his arms hither and thither. Then he exclaimed facetiously: 'Mosquito guerrilla warfare. I can't bear it. I'm off.' And he rose, took his leave of me and went away.

Next day I had to admit that the Special Correspondent was right. If one did not dig in the 'mine of news' that was Fort Lamy, everything was exactly as it had been in the mining areas before digging had started: sunshine, calm, normality. The French quarter had been conceived with the spaciousness of Parisian town planning: vast circular open spaces adorned with large decorative fountains; broad shady avenues flanked by the gardens of handsome villas and *de luxe* hotels. Then the African quarter: clay walls, a maze of sandy paths between huts with thatched roofs, swarms of people and incessant comings and goings. As in the empty, silent French quarter, so also in the crowded, noisy African quarter, calm and normality seemed really to prevail, at any rate in appearance. Certainly one would have to dig. But for the purpose of digging, was there not already the Special Correspondent?

A wide, shady avenue divides the famous, immense market, trading centre of the Chad, into two principal sectors: to the left, that of foodstuffs, sold mainly by women; to the right, manufactured goods, presented chiefly by men. This division probably corresponds to analogous economic functions in the family and tribal communities. To the women, the victualling; to the men, the manufacture. We began with the feminine sector, in which a huge, airy, very crowded marquee provides shade and protection from the fierce African sun for the goods which are in a high degree perishable. We started to circulate idly amongst the crowd, looking and pretending to be searching for something. Here were vegetables and fruits, fresh and of fine quality; seeds, flour, grain of indescribable variety, of all sorts of colours, in little pyramids like the powders in paint-shops; fish from the Chari and the Logone, already fried and already smelling strong; blackish pieces of meat covered with flies; poultry, young goats, lambs, alive and in a sorry state, tied up and thrown on the ground among the feet of the buyers. The goods, to tell the truth, were much the same as can be seen in all the markets in the world. It was the saleswomen, if anything, who were different.

For the most part they were young, good-looking women, their hair parted into endless little thin tresses springing from their heads over their foreheads, their cheeks and the backs of their necks. Some of them had rings in the septa of their noses. Bright-coloured materials were closely wound round them from their breasts to their ankles. They squatted on the ground in front of their wares, looking rapturous or sleepy; but they woke up at once at the bid of a buyer, with an intensity of participation that seemed to go beyond the mere pursuit of profit and to attain the mysterious region of the desire for power. And thus one saw that these same women, with the revolutions of the Third World, would be installed – without rings in their noses, without little tresses of hair, without materials of barbaric design, but with the same shrewd, zealous participation – in modern, air-conditioned offices, devoting themselves to the wholesale distribution of these same cereals, of this same fruit, of this same meat as they strove to sell here, retail, in a still depressed economy.

Curiously enough, these same reflections did not take shape in my mind in the sector where manufactured goods were put up for sale by the men. As for the traders, draped in white and standing behind the merchandise set out on stalls in the manner of the Oriental bazaar, it was difficult to imagine them no longer unoccupied and on the alert but efficient and rational, sitting at European desks in bureaucratic offices. Strange to say, it was precisely because the women were, or seemed to be, more picturesque that one imagined their transformation would be more radical. Also because to the social and economic revolution will be added that of the women, which in the Third World is perhaps the newest and most overpowering.

It is certain, however, that in the passage from the open-air market to the planned economy something will be lost, irreparably. For example, the wonderful exhibitions of cosmetics. No more shall we see the blond sparkle of innumerable bottles adorned with improbable silvery labels. The bottles look like those of the Parisian perfumers of some decades ago. Possibly they were bought up and then refilled, in Cairo or in the Lebanon, with local lotions and scents made specially for the clientele of Black Africa.

We went back into the avenue; and there we came upon a row of truly peculiar women. Their little tresses stood upright like pins on a pincushion, on top of shaven skulls; and they had curious symmetrical scars on their cheeks. They were crouching on the ground, exhausted, not selling anything; they were perhaps waiting for the rickety bus to take them back to some remote village or other, hidden away in the bush. We made an agreement, in the customary way, to take a photograph of them; we paid, and then got ready to take it; but a voice stopped us. 'Why are you taking a photograph of these women? In your own country you wouldn't allow us to do that.'

There were three young men, probably students, reproaching us with nationalist severity. We replied that in our country anybody photographed anybody. They shrugged their shoulders and told us that we were 'neo-colonialists'. But suddenly the Special Correspondent popped out from somewhere or other. 'Photographs, eh?' he said. 'So we're still at that stage? I'll say good-bye, I'm leaving. Here at Fort Lamy there's nothing to be done. I'm going to Tripoli. I'm told it's a veritable mine of news. One has only to dig . . .'